SM0000 4094
3/01

0335203957

Current Titles

Concepts in the Social Sciences

Structuration

John Parker

Open University Press
Buckingham · Philadelphia

Open University Press
Celtic Court
22 Ballmoor
Buckingham
MK18 1XW

email: enquiries@openup.co.uk
world wide web: http://www.openup.co.uk

and 325 Chestnut Street
Philadelphia, PA 19106, USA

First Published 2000

A catalogue record of this book is available from the British Library

ISBN 0 335 20395 7 (hb)   0 335 20394 9 (pb)

Library of Congress Cataloging-in-Publication Data
Parker, John, 1946–
      Structuration/John Parker.
         p.   cm. — (Concepts in the social sciences)
      Includes bibliographical references and index.
      ISBN 0-335-20395-7 — ISBN 0-335-20394-9 (pbk.)
      1. Sociology–Methodology. 2. Social structure. 3. Structuralism.
         I. Title. II. Series.
      HM511.P37 2000
      301'.01—dc21   00-037513

Typeset by Type Study, Scarborough, North Yorkshire
Printed in Great Britain by St Edmundsbury Press, Bury St Edmunds

*To the students of Further Social Theory at
University of Wales, Swansea, between 1984 and 1999*

Contents

Preface and Acknowledgements

The term structuration will have come to the attention of all students of the social and historical sciences as well as many in the humanities. That is because they are all involved in studying phenomena which, though exerting power over human beings (social structures, institutions, cultural traditions, genres, styles, fashions etc.), are also the products of human beings. This relationship between the subjective powers of human agents and the objective powers of the realities they have a hand in producing is central to any attempt to understand how such structures are produced, that is, their structuration.

Though the term is used in this general way to refer to the forming of structures, its prominence as a term is due to its special use by Giddens in his 'structuration' theory. This repudiates 'dualism', that is any approach to the objective and subjective contributions to structures as different in kind. 'Structuration' theory accounts for the structuration of social structures and systems by conceptualizing the relation between the subjective powers of human agents and the objective powers of the structures they produce, as one of 'duality'; there is no difference of kind. This book considers the perennial and general problem of the structuration of such structures and asks whether 'structuration' theory and its central idea, the 'duality of structure', is of any use in solving the problem. The discussion focuses attention on the critics of 'structuration' theory who defend dualism, and makes suggestions about how such problems ought to be tackled.

Part One describes the context in the early 1970s when the term was introduced and explains why it attracted so much attention, particularly in the context of Giddens's 'structuration' theory. This theory was a cultural product satisfying certain emotional and political needs at a particular moment. The question of intellectual generations is raised. The theory also has a particular logical character which needs to be displayed. I describe the theoretical debates and innovations which preceded it and provided the theoretical resources used by the 'structuration' theorists.

To clear a path through the issues, I focus on only four major social theorists. Part Two considers the major contributors to 'structuration' theory, Bourdieu and Giddens. Part Three deals with the criticisms and alternatives proposed by Archer and Mouzelis. These chapters can be read separately as introductions to the work of each author. In the available space it is only possible to focus on how they conceptualize processes of structuration. However, I try to show how their ideas about structuration arise in the context of their other work.

The question of the usefulness of the concept of structuration will be decided by determining the contribution it makes to understanding the establishment of enduring, patterned forms of social relations and practices, and the contribution of human agents to such establishments. Unless one thinks like some postmodernists that this is impossible in principle, historical sociology is the proper testing ground for the notion of structuration and for sociology itself. The book concludes by discussing recent developments in historical sociology, particularly those of Mann and Runciman. Though not contributing directly to the debate over 'structuration' theory, they nevertheless contribute to a post-'structurationist' sociology.

I believe that the moment of 'structuration' theory passed some time ago. It still figures prominently in routine social theoretical talk, but its force is only that of a tired conventional wisdom. The main purpose of this book is to contribute to making the dualist alternatives to 'structuration' theory better known. I hope readers will feel that they can appreciate the energy, technical accomplishment and attraction of 'structuration' theory, but without being seduced by it. It is now an important part of everyone's social theoretical legacy.

I would like to thank those members of the Department of Sociology and Anthropology at Swansea who covered my administrative duties during a semester's study leave when the bulk of the book was written. Reg Byron, as head of department, was suitably encouraging as the project took shape. Len Mars and Tom Parker read chapters at different stages of development and gave helpful advice. I am especially grateful to Hilary Stanworth who edited the whole thing, ensuring I kept to the word limit and saving me from all sorts of carelessness. It was a pleasure working with Justin Vaughan, Gaynor Clements and Viv Cracknell at Open University Press.

PART ONE
Contexts

Introduction

Approaching 'structuration' sociologically

During the last quarter of the twentieth century the use of the term structuration has become routine in anglophone social science. Introduced in 1973 by Anthony Giddens in a discussion of the processes of class formation, it rapidly entered the vocabulary of teachers and students of sociology and those humanities interested in using social theory (Giddens 1973). As an historical phenomenon, the origins and rise to such prominence of the concept, and interest in the problems it alludes to, can be usefully approached as a problem for the sociology of culture and knowledge. Concepts are developed in historical circumstances, by specific people who are socially located in institutional environments and configurations of power and conflicting interests. The invention of concepts and theories is a practice which, like any practice, has its methods, but it is questionable how sufficient these are to explain what is produced by using them. Theoretical reasoning is not sufficient to explain what it is used to produce. The approach taken here is that reason is not sufficiently powerful to secure its independence from non-rational forces which also shape theoretical developments. To explain the origin of the concept of 'structuration' we must refer to such 'external' forces, in particular the forces of the emotions and a whole catalogue of possible social interests (Kilminster 1991; Clegg 1992). These are forged and reforged in the relentlessness of social competition. It will help us get to grips with the concept if we approach it from the point of view of the sociology of culture, treating it as an object of contested cultural value. This will require using a battery of sociological concepts such as interests, markets, generations, alliances, leadership roles, intellectuals, educational hierarchies, classes, opportunity structures, intellectual fields, occupational orders, carrier strata and so on.

This book is written for, and from the point of view of, ordinary teachers and students in western higher education: what we have to do is put ourselves in the shoes of people like ourselves between, say, 1964 and 1974. This is not the point of view of intellectual heroes, or the avant-garde, but of an expanding intellectual sub-elite of consumers seeking guidance, trying to keep up to date, preparing courses, writing essays, and so on – much as you do yourself. However, ordinary consumers like you play more than a passive role in theory development. Their relationship with theory is not simply required by an academic curriculum, but animated by the experience of specific events and conditions occurring in contemporary society.

In the late 1960s there was intense demand for theory which could help make sense of current circumstances. Interest in theory was not simply a response to dull academic compulsion. It was part of a major redistribution of generational power and cultural change which were unintended effects of the liberal-democratic policies of western states following World War Two. The promise of rising living standards, full employment, upward social mobility through educational achievement, and the welfare state had addressed the social imagination of 1945, conditioned by war and before that the mass unemployment of the 1930s. But for the first postwar generation, this definition of the good life was not as appealing as it was for their parents. By the early 1960s the young people entering higher education felt that their parents' utopia did not live up to its egalitarian promise. There had to be more to a worthwhile personal life than material comfort and safety. More importantly, the continued existence of inequalities of class, race, gender, ethnicity and age contradicted the claim to legitimacy of the rich democracies. The civil rights movement in the United States and a new wave of feminism were symptomatic. As was the younger generation's critique of western governments' opposition to national liberation movements and communist regimes. The Vietnam War, impacting directly on the personal lives of American youth, symbolized the illegitimacy of the existing order. Faced with this crisis the field of social theory expanded and became full of conflict about which sort of theory could cope.

Thus, during the 1960s, knowledge of theory became simultaneously less optional and more difficult because of the explosion of alternatives. Theory became exciting, socially valuable and morally compelling; to be good at it commanded high status. But the stakes were high. Would-be leaders had to present their innovations in a form which would attract followers. Emphasizing the recognizability and accessibility of their ideas risked downplaying their innovation. Stressing a theory's radicality and unfamiliarity courted charges of obscurantism. Theory's consumers also faced dangers as they were pushed to make choices on the basis of limited knowledge, thereby threatening to overreach or make fools of themselves. Those who did not welcome this might withhold commitment, but then risked failing to achieve the very theoretical purchase on contemporary realities which motivated their involvement with theory in the first place.

How does structuration stand in this light? Most importantly, the moment of 'structuration' theory came in the early 1970s *after* a decade of theoretical expansion and confusion. I suggest it allowed intellectual leaders to offer innovation in a form which could be recognized – though not always *as* innovation. The two leading 'structurationists', Giddens and Bourdieu, have both had their originality questioned and both have made conspicuous efforts to popularize their ideas, though neither has entirely escaped the charge of obscurantism. From the consumers' perspective, 'structuration' facilitated orientation to the field, allowing them to satisfy the demand that they have something to say about theory. It represented a relatively under-committing commitment; positions may be adopted in a way which makes them easy to give up, and little is actually given up when taking a position in the first place. The intellectual method, which encourages this mode of engagement with the demands of theory, will be considered later. Here I stress that 'structuration' theory offered a kind of safe bet in a period when consumers were being required to take intellectual risks (Bauman 1989: 35).

After offering some preliminary definitions, the rest of this chapter will place the emergence and establishment of the term, and the associated concepts to which it is used to refer, in a cultural and institutional context, to identify the interests it served, and the alternatives to which it seemed preferable. What were and are the risks of contemporary social theory against which 'structuration' theory seemed to offer some protection?

The two meanings of structuration

Having briefly considered the development of 'structuration' theory as an historical and cultural event, it is now necessary to provide some preliminary discussion of definitions. The term structuration has been used in two related ways. First it has been used to refer to the generation of structures. Giddens says structuration 'refers abstractly to the dynamic process whereby structures come into being' (Giddens 1976: 121). Anyone interested in establishing the origins of structures is therefore interested in their structuration. There is nothing technical or specifically sociological about this definition. One can imagine, say, biologists, physical geographers, plastics engineers, scaffolders, or the bakers of cakes using the term. It has application irrespective of the kinds of structures, or the kinds of structuring processes, being investigated. But it always refers to such *structure-producing processes*. This first usage can be translated as 'structuring process' without any loss of meaning. As a 'process' concept it must refer to some series of events with temporal duration, among which there are systematic relations with the cumulative effects which explain the existence of the structure in question.

It follows that the concept only has purchase if it is accepted that there is a 'structure' of some sort to be explained in the first place. Anything can be thought of as a structure provided it is conceptualized as composed of relations between parts. *Structures* are identified by structural analysis, that is the breaking down of the object into relations between components. Structural analysis tries to understand complex realities by trying out different ideas about the nature of their important components and the relations between them. The complex objects of the sciences (sociology, biology, linguistics, chemistry, physics and so on) are rendered intelligible by using appropriate abstractions which concentrate attention on a relatively few elements which promise to reveal how the complex object works. In sociology, for example, competing class theories offer sets of abstractions with which to represent structures of systematically organized hierarchies of power and opportunity. Once represented as such, and given certain assumptions about such things as the perception of interests, these theories provide a powerful basis for explaining a wide range of cultural, political and possibly psychological characteristics of the social worlds in question. Theoretical structures (e.g. as in theories of class structure) are produced to help us understand the world, but once postulated and substantiated (e.g. empirical implications of class theories are shown to hold in fact) those same structures may invite the investigation of their origination or structuration. Thus at the heart of this first use of the term is the recognition that structures are not eternal, but exist in historical time and are the products of historical processes. Structuration refers to these processes.

The second use of structuration, however, is specific to a *particular kind of solution* to the problem of structuration as that exists for the social sciences. It is this use which Giddens adopts, as a special piece of theoretical vocabulary, for his version of 'structuration' theory. This special use arises from the particular nature of the structures of social reality. On the one hand social reality is made up of structures of various kinds – that is complex *wholes* composed of relations between components, such as institutions, belief systems and stratification systems. These have the properties and duration which we think of as 'historical'. Each is the product of historical processes of structuration, in the first sense just discussed. On the other hand, such structures are populated by human beings whose lives are organized by them. It is human beings who occupy the roles in institutions, who believe the beliefs, or are positioned in relations of inequality. This distinction between the *parts* of social structures and the *human material* is fundamental to social reality.

When we explain the structuration of social structures we have to consider the relations between these two different kinds of material, the social-structural and the human. Were the human to be thought of as just so much objective biological matter then structuration of social structures could be explained in much the same way as one might explain a natural process such as weather patterns. But if the human material is thought of, not simply as objective, but as having some powers of structuration itself, then the explanation of social structures must be rather different. These creatures would have to be given their due weight as subjective agents, in any explanatory use of, or attempts to explain the origins of, structures. As subjects, humans are defined as having at least the potential to resist and manipulate structural constraints, and sometimes to use genuinely creative powers to innovate and transform the structural conditions of their social existence. In short they are, at least potentially, *agents*, that is beings with some responsibility for shaping the social conditions of existence.

In general, social theory has felt it necessary at least to face up to the suggestion of human agency, if only to reject it. In fact it is hardly ever rejected outright. It is usually assumed that the human sciences must allow for the operation of human agency whenever accounting for the effects or origins of structures. Some sort of relation has to been made between the objective force of social structures and the powers of agency of the human material. If, for example, we wanted to explain what people did, by deriving their activity from a class structure, we must at the same time acknowledge that the class structure can be derived from their activity. Much more needs to be said about this view of human agents and structures and its relevance for the human sciences, but for the moment it is sufficient to say that the structuration of social structures has to relate structure to agency, if humans are not simply objects.

The objectivity of social structures and the subjectivity of the human material are the most fundamental elements of the solution to the problem of structuration as it is encountered in the human sciences. The solution requires an account of how they interact as structure-producing forces. In the standard language, the contributions of objective (i.e. where no human agency is exercised) and subjective (i.e. those requiring the exercise of agency) powers of structuring have to be recognized. Neither the objective nor the subjective is sufficient alone. This widely accepted position stands opposed to *objectivism*, which holds that no reference to subjects is required, and to *subjectivism*, which holds that no reference to objects is required.

However, there is an important technical implication of this balancing of the objective and the subjective and that is that they are not simply related by their contribution to the origination of a third party, structure, but are mutually dependent. They are, in some way, conditions of each other. Just as objective and constraining social structures are said to be constituted, to some degree, by the subjective powers of agency of human actors, so these very powers of agency are said to be constituted in some way by objective social structures. It is this interdependence which has led Giddens to suggest the second sense of 'structuration', claiming that it implies rejection of the dualism of object and subject. Dualism is the form of thinking in which basic categories are regarded as logically exclusive of each other. In this case objects cannot be subjects and vice versa. The concept of 'structuration', in the sense specific to

Objectivism (Structuralism)	v.	Objects **related** to subjects (structures) + (agency) How? *Either*	v.	**Subjectivism** (Humanism)
objects reduce subjects: no agency		(a) Dualism; **non-identity** relation e.g. Lockwood, Archer, Weber, Mouzelis. *Or* (b) Duality; **identity** of structure and agency i.e. Giddens's concept of '*structuration*'		subjects reduce objects: no structure

Figure 1.1   The three basic ways of accounting for structuration

Giddens's 'structuration' theory, involves thinking of objectivity and subjectivity with respect to the formation of structures, as constitutive of each other, and hence as not being logically exclusive. For him the relation between structure and agency is one of 'duality', not dualism. As we shall see, Giddens's claim that his sense necessarily follows from the interdependence of subjects and objects in social reality is a matter of dispute, to put it mildly!

The critics of Giddens, discussed in Part Three, hold that to explain the structuration of social structures by recognizing both the contributions of objective processes and human powers of agency does not necessitate abandoning the dualism of structure (object) and agency (subject). Dualism asserts the non-identity of the two, whereas Giddens asserts their identity (Craib 1986). So, to recapitulate, in the first sense the term structuration refers to *the processes involved in producing structures*. In the social sciences, where the *interdependence of structure and agency in accounting for the production of social structures* is generally accepted, the question is one of how they are related. 'Structuration' in the second sense refers to the *'duality', or identity of structure and agency,* proposed by Giddens. From now on when using the word with this sense it will have quotation marks! All sociologists are interested in accounting for social structures and almost all accept the interdependence of structure and agency. But it is wrong to say that because this is so 'we are all "structurationists" now', because not everyone accepts Giddens's way of relating the two. The debate is no longer about *whether* structure and agency are related, but

about the *nature* of that relation – should it be one of identity or
non-identity? (Figure 1.1 summarizes the situation.) This book concentrates on just this issue.

The theory of the 1960s; the foundations for 'structuration' theory

We have seen that the term structuration entered the vocabulary
of social theory during the mid-1970s after a decade characterized
by intense social theoretical activity motivated by moral and political interests. This activity took academics (and students) of the late
1960s and early 1970s in a variety of different directions. Marxist
theories of revolution, both objectivist and structuralist (the capitalist system revolutionizes itself), and subjectivist and humanist
(the proletariat revolutionizes capitalism when it wants to), were
joined by non-Marxist theories of action and interaction (Weber,
Symbolic Interactionism, Ethnomethodology) which emphasized
constructive, creative agency and the 'negotiated' character of
social life. All promised insight into the structuration of structures
which might be used to understand history, while the non-structuralist ones suggested that people could perhaps take the reins and
produce new and better structures for themselves.

Riding on the back of the concern with change and conflict was
interest in the power of culture. That change and political effectiveness depended in some way on meaning was implicit in all non-
structuralist theories which assigned some weight to subjectivity in
their accounts of the origins of structures. Humanist Marxism
focused on the power of ideology and the possibilities for politically effective criticism, while action theories concentrated on how
language was used creatively in interaction, to achieve cooperation
and legitimacy. However, these approaches all treated the consciousness of human beings and the hermeneutic processes of
interpretation as the source of meaning. This was opposed by
French structuralism, which saw meaning as a product of objective
semiotic processes, thereby subordinating the subjectivity and consciousness of human actors to the meaning-producing mechanisms
claimed for culture itself. French structuralism interested the mid-
1960s generation of students trying to understand social change,
because of its claims to reveal cultural forms' hidden meanings. But
it denied the history-producing power of human agency and indeed
the reality of history itself (Clarke 1981; Anderson 1983).

What all of the above positions seemed to offer the new 1960s academic generation were ways of breaking with the established form of theory which had developed in the early postwar years. This suggested that to understand society sociology should identify what it needed to function efficiently. It claimed that objective social structures, as self-producing mechanisms, governed human social existence, and that sociology should aim to become a deterministic natural science. In particular it interpreted history as a natural process of progressive modernization. Why this type of theory was felt inadequate to meet the needs of the 1960s will be discussed in the next chapter.

By the early 1970s, commentators presented the state of theory in terms of a contrast between an 'orthodox consensus' around functionalism, modernization and scientism, established in the 1950s, and an 'unorthodox dissensus' comprised of the variety of disunited positions mentioned above, whose only basis for unity was a preoccupation with conflict and their opposition to orthodoxy (Atkinson 1971; Bernstein 1976; Giddens 1987: 54). I hinted earlier that the plurality of positions available (the division between the orthodox and the unorthodox and the great variety within the latter) could be stressful, particularly for 'ordinary consumers'. Whichever stand they took had costs and benefits. They could embrace and try to defend 'orthodoxy'. They could opt enthusiastically for one of the new alternatives, and wage theoretical war on its competitors. They might wander among the competitors, exploring them and enjoying the variety, ignoring the incompatibilities. They might keep their heads down, perhaps carrying on with 'research', in the realistic, if slightly cynical, hope that the theoretical storms would sooner or later blow themselves out. The remaining alternative, probably too ambitious for the 'ordinary' consumer, was to size up the competitors and construct a critical synthesis of them. This was the task which Bourdieu and Giddens set themselves and which led to 'structuration'.

Their primary move involved jettisoning the orthodox/unorthodox divide. Instead of 'orthodoxy versus the rest', they simplified the field by conceptualizing it as riven by the opposition between objectivism and subjectivism or 'structure and agency'. They substituted a philosophical opposition between ontologies for the politically loaded opposing of 'orthodoxy' by 'radical alternative(s)'. This preliminary 'mapping' gave additional purchase on the field which could then be worked on using the preferred method, namely synthesizing. The incompatibility of approaches which confined themselves to either objective or subjective accounts was to be overcome by extracting elements from each side which could be made to work in harmony. The 'structurationist' path carried the price of polymathic scholarship, but offered the prize of a comprehensive, inclusive, integrated position. Such a position offered the security of not having to reject anything lock, stock and barrel; it was open, and found a use for something from almost all of the competitors (Clegg 1992: 146–7). Its 'democratic' inclusiveness was achieved through its rather 'aristocratic' imposition of an integrating, superordinate vision transcending the limitations of each of the contributing positions. It sought to achieve a single authoritative resolution of theoretical conflict through the exercise of reason (Barrell 1983).

Thus, despite its critical and constructive energy, this synthesizing response to the period of theoretical expansion and pluralization was in one sense conservative. Though addressing ontological choices, the synthetic method sought to save the ideal of 'truth' from the relativising effects of theoretical pluralization, as well as from actual arguments for the relativity of truth made by some among the plurality. Achieving the classic intellectual ideal of an integrated theoretical basis for the social sciences was the goal (Kilminster 1991: 75). The moment of 'structuration' theory, combining the concern with the historical character of structures with the synthesizing of objective and subjective approaches within the human sciences, was part of a tendency to bring those sciences to some sort of order. It satisfied an ecumenical impulse, and offered the possibility of continuity between the old theory world of the 'orthodox consensus' and a new world, built with elements selectively appropriated from the opponents of that consensus. Whatever the intentions and carefulness of the intellectual leaders of the 'structuration' movement, their very success, both academically and commercially, is testament to the existence of a huge demand for the authoritative work of those who had the ability to shoulder the massive scholarly and intellectual burdens required to construct the desired synthesis. 'Structuration' demanded rare intellectual creativity and by the same token encouraged dependency among those who, while experiencing the desire for a comprehensive and inclusive position, were not in a position to create it for themselves. An alliance was formed between a generation of intellectual leaders who came to their full powers in the early 1960s (Giddens,

b. 1938; Bourdieu, b. 1930) and a generation of students entering higher education social science courses in unprecedented numbers from the late 1960s on. The leaders supplied what was required to contain theoretical overload.

This chapter has briefly shown that 'structuration' theory arose out of a particular social and theoretical context. The next two chapters will look at the latter in more detail. They will (a) elaborate why major examples of the orthodox consensus came to be felt to be unsatisfactory, and (b) show how the range of moves that were made by those within the unorthodox dissensus provided ideas for Bourdieu and Giddens to draw upon, but also difficulties for them to resolve. The most basic difficulty the 'structurationists' had to resolve was creating a theoretical position that gave *sufficient* weight to *both* structure and agency. They were committed to the historical agency of human beings and the moral dignity that implies. History could be made. But they also had a strong sense of objective structural constraints on agency. History could not be made at will. All the existing positions, though offering them material to work with, tended in the end to overemphasize, or eradicate, structure or agency.

2

The Structurationist Imagination and the Making of History

Structuration as the central problem for social theory

In this chapter and the next, I am going to discuss social theoretical developments which anticipated the contributions of Bourdieu and Giddens to the analysis of structuration. As I suggested in the previous chapter, their synthetic projects found a ready market. That the central problem for social theory was somehow to relate structure and agency was by then a commonplace. Moreover, the theoretical resources which they brought together in their syntheses were already familiar, at least in outline. Before we can consider these resources in any detail, and the development of the idea of 'structuration' in the second sense (and Giddens's particular version of 'structuration' theory), we must first consider why this problem should have seemed so obviously important. Why was it necessary to solve it? The answer is to be found by considering why structuration, in the first sense (to which 'structuration' in the second sense is a kind of answer), should have become the central problem for social theory in the 1960s.

At that time, although the term structuration was not current, the concept in the first sense was very familiar. The concern to specify the processes involved in the formation of historical structures was central to classical sociology's exploration of the formation and structure of modern society. So to the extent that sociology's *raison d'être* has always been the explanation of a certain sort of structure, structuration is nothing other than its

central problem. Since sociology's task is to account for the reproduction and transformation of phenomena, which being social are
necessarily relational and therefore structured, then the sociological imagination must have the concept of structuration at its
core.

Sociology was invented to supply the conceptual resources for
understanding the specific historical changes of social structure
associated with the process of modernization. However, its general
theories of structural change, developed to deal with the social consequences of the industrialization of western Europe, have been
repeatedly criticized and revised in response to subsequent changes
and application to other cases. Theories of social structural formation are continually put under pressure by the experience of
events and emergent patterns. Predictions fail, the unpredicted
impresses itself, the relative power of causal factors has to be re-
evaluated, new insights are discovered into the way elements of
structures are related. Innovation emerges out of the confrontation
between theory and experience. Thus the episode of theoretical
development we are dealing with in the early 1970s was not unique
but a normal response to changes which current theories appeared
unable to explain. Throughout the history of sociology, bouts of
structuration theorizing have been triggered by this sort of contradictory experience.

The experience of the postwar generation, touched on in the last
chapter, was the trigger for the new wave of theorizing about structural formation and transformation, or what amounts to the same
thing, theories of history, which resulted in Bourdieu and Giddens's
'structuration' theory in the early 1970s. The extraordinary logic of
the then orthodox theory of historical development, as much as the
dramatic nature of real-world events, contributed to the strong
sense of contradiction between the two which fuelled the renewed
interest in the problem of history. The debate about structuration
is a debate about what form a general theory of historical change
should take.

Normative integration and systems functionalism

'Modernization theory' was the orthodox theory whose unpopu-
larity increased as its shortcomings rapidly became more evident.
It tried to address historical change within the frame of reference
of a type of functionalism referred to as 'systems' or 'normative'

functionalism of which Parsons was the chief architect. Though modernization theory sought to revive nineteeth-century social evolutionism, it must be understood within the functionalist context which Parsons developed to answer what was for him social theory's central question, namely the 'problem of social order'. Parsons was inspired by Durkheim, who asked how complex, highly individualized, modern industrial societies cohered, concluding that there was a force strong enough to counteract the 'centrifugal tendencies' of the division of labour, which made people increasingly different from one another. He found this force, which maintained 'social solidarity', in commonly held moral values which transcended the differences arising from the differentiating effects of the industrialization of work. *For Durkheim and Parsons the problem for social theory is to provide the concepts for analysing how the forces of differentiation are related to the forces of integration in functioning social orders.*

To solve the central issue of how the integration of a social system is reproduced, Parsons adopted the 'action frame of reference'. He clearly accepted that structuration required structure and agency to be related. He conceptualized the populations of societies as 'actors' who were free to make choices about desired *ends* and the *means* to achieve them. This freedom was potentially disintegrating, so integration was to be explained by whatever constrained actors to choose to act in ways which maintained social order. Parsons rejected attempts to make sociology scientific by disregarding human subjectivity. He wanted a sociology which fully accepted that individual actors were self-directing and had the freedom to act voluntarily. So the solution to the problem of integration lay in whatever constrained the way actors make choices. He criticized early utilitarian theories of action which thought of 'choosing' solely in terms of the application of empirical knowledge by rational individuals, because they only partially explained how actors choose the 'means' for achieving their ends, and failed entirely to explain the choice of ends. Utilitarianism left these 'random', thereby threatening integration. That individual actors apply more or less accurate *knowledge*, more or less *rationally*, does not explain social order. Parsons saw that some additional element was required to constrain the choice of ends and the choice between equally practical and rational means.

The additional element, which 'de-randomizes' the choosing of ends and maintains integration, Parsons calls the '*normative*'. This refers to the socially provided values people use when making qualitative judgements. Parsons argued that Durkheim and Weber, and the social sciences generally, had converged on the idea that moral and aesthetic values were fundamental for explaining human action and social order (Parsons [1937]1968). Parsons identified agreement about two major issues. First, since action involves value judgements, but individual actors cannot be the source of values, the freedom to act depends on being supplied with values by a society to which the actor belongs. Socialization is the process which ensures that individual actors have the values they need and are thereby socially integrated. Second, values vary in their generality such that at the highest level there are 'ultimate values', to which all the different kinds of action generated by the forces of differentiation can be referred. Culture (more specifically, religion) overarches the different institutions and occupations, providing the basic terms for their coordination and hence integration.

Parsons's brilliant synthesis of non-Marxist classical social theory distinguishes between the problem of how actors relate to each other and the problem of how the different parts of a society are related. Cultural values link these two kinds of relations – those between actors, and those between institutions, practices, or divisions of labour. As we shall see, the attempt to link the two kinds of relations is of fundamental importance. However, though Parsons began by insisting on a fully 'voluntaristic' social theory, treating action as genuinely free, his primary interest in the integration of functioning social orders and the relations between the parts of any society quickly sidelined the 'voluntaristic' requirement. He emphasized the predictability rather than the variation of ends actors might seek even within a unified culture. The result is an 'overintegrated' vision of society. Relations between choice-making actors become just one more component of social systems. The two kinds of relations are related by having one determining the other, and Parsons slides towards objectivism.

Though Parsons continued to use the terms 'action' and 'actor' as he developed his functionalist account of social systems, it became difficult to maintain the meanings they had in his earlier critique of utilitarian action theories. Actors' autonomy is massively reduced to the point where they merely provide the energy required to satisfy the expectations of social roles. They are agents only in the sense of 'representatives' of the social roles and positions to which they have been 'allocated'. As 'functionaries' they play virtually no part in the formation of expectations. This socio-logical determinism follows from thinking of societies as entities with self-forming, self-regulating processes, which are able to act for themselves. These processes explain why there are the positions and roles there are, and how people are formed to occupy them.

It is here we encounter Parsons's full-blown systems functional-ism which is the target of 'structurationist' criticism. Its basic idea is that societies have 'functional prerequisites' or necessary con-ditions of existence (Bershady 1973; Craib 1992a; Layder 1994; Scott 1995; Baert 1998). Roles and institutions exist because they supply these necessary conditions, which are of two kinds: those dependent on relations with the external environment, and those dependent on relations internal to the system itself. Supplying the necessary conditions involves choosing appropriate ends and means for achieving them. Parsons suggests that specialized insti-tutions develop to supply either means or ends for solving internal or external problems. There are therefore four 'prerequisites': **A**daptation (means/external), **G**oal attainment (ends/external), **I**ntegration (means/internal) and **L**atency (ends/internal) (**AGIL**). So, for example, markets supply scarce resources ('means') from the external environment ('adaptation') and governments decide about 'ends' ('goal attainment'). Parsons's argument is that the components of societies exist to contribute in a complementary way to the continued existence of the whole.

Modernization theory and evolutionism

For systems functionalism, the relation between the parts needed for the survival of society is the atemporal one of simultaneous interdependence. However, implicit in the theory is an historical process of specialization and institutional development. This is the central plank of modernization theory, which tried to overcome the ahistorical character of systems functionalism. In line with nine-teenth-century social evolutionism, it argues that because develop-ment is survival-driven, the future can be predicted. Development is governed by law-like processes, which involve the improvement of the technical capacity to solve problems. This capacity depends on two linked factors: the development of scientific knowledge and technology and the increasing horizontal differentiation of the div-ision of labour. The development of industrial means of produc-tion, education systems to cultivate the people's abilities, effective motivation, rewards and allocation methods (centring on money and markets), and universalistic values enshrined in democracy, bureaucracy and rational law, was supposed to result in a heady combination of efficiency, freedom from want, justice and individual self-fulfilment.

There are a number of fundamental features of modernization theory. It is *universalistic and deterministic*. Because the above pattern of institutional developments offers enhanced survival capacity, it sees a general tendency for all societies to evolve them. There is therefore only one future and history is 'closed'. Substantively in Parsons's influential version that future is American. The United States is celebrated as the 'new lead society' whose present is other countries' future (Parsons 1966, 1971).

Modernization theory is also *ethical naturalistic*. Values are derived from what social science tells us about the survival requirements of society. The logic of the argument is thoroughly positivist; the hand dealt us by the *objective nature* of historical development is warmly embraced. The only possibility is the best possibility! Modernist naturalism treats history as closed, predictable and unopposable, but also as morally desirable. Any difference between the reality of history and our ideals for the future is collapsed. The moral imagination of modernization theory is therefore restricted.

It is also *normative functionalist*. Modernization happens when individuals are constrained by appropriate socialization, motivated by appropriate rewards, and allocated to roles suited to their skills and dispositions. There is a fundamental similarity of the interests of all individuals seeking to satisfy their 'need-dispositions'. In addition, the coordination of the institutional fabric of society is said to take place at the level of the most general and 'ultimate' values. Values therefore 'integrate' relations between the institutional parts of a society and, via the socialization process, 'integrate' individuals with each other and into their social positions in institutions. Moreover, cultural consensus among individuals within cultures is extended to convergence between different cultures as each succumbs to the survival benefits of the value-complex of modernity.

In short, modernization theory recommends what it regards as coming about whether we like it or not. The functional requirements of all societies and the interests of all individuals will be best served by encouraging the development of the most inclusive social institutions. Democratic states, market relations, voluntary associations, meritocratic education, achievement orientation, impersonal administration and rational law form a set of institutions which are conducive to personal liberty and to the effective use of individuals for meeting functional requirements. The ideological character of this is pretty obvious, excused perhaps by its proponents' optimistic belief in and desire to bolster democracy and rationality after fascism's recent defeat.

The denial of system contradictions and the reification of social reality

Two of the primary characteristics of modernization theory (the historical form of systems functionalism) were fundamental for the emergence of the structuration problematic. The first is its belief that *modernization promises the prospect of an optimally integrated social order, devoid of systemic contradictions.* Change continues, but only in the form of gains in efficiency and survival capacity that are always being sought. No potential for disintegration is recognized once the fully integrated set of modern institutions is established. Neither individuals, nor the social system itself, are credited with system-changing powers.

Modernization theory's second significant feature is that *the human individuals who inhabit social systems are treated as functional resources for the system.* They are sources of energy for doing what is functionally necessary, but are not historically significant actors, capable of influencing the direction of change, that is, the structuration of structures. The result is that though the theory recognizes that social reality is materially made up of human beings, they are not really regarded as actors, except in the sense of fulfilling the requirements of roles. As I said earlier, they are 'functionaries', not actors in the strong sense of being embodied selves capable of self-direction and intentionality. If we take reference to fully-fledged actors as a test of the realism of social theory, then modernization/systems functionalist theory can be accused of 'reification' (Mouzelis 1995: 78–9). The role of human actors in the historical process is virtually eliminated and the attempt to relate structure and agency evaporates.

Absent mechanisms and/or agents of history

As I suggested in the last chapter, by the 1960s the USA was increasingly seen as an inequalitarian state whose exploitative relations with the third world suggested that modern societies were more of a problem than a solution for many people. The Vietnam War and the American civil rights movement deflated the American modernist balloon and made the idea that there was only an American-shaped future, even if true, decreasingly attractive. There were strong political, moral and intellectual motives to find an alternative to the naturalism of modernization theory. The desire for an alternative future, the recognition of the value of cultural difference and conflicts of values and interests, and the defence of the historical importance of human actors were the three principles which motivated the critique.

As social theory, modernization theory and systems functionalism shared a major weakness. Modernizing development involves a series of progressive changes, and functioning societies require constant renewal of their conditions of existence, so there has to be some directing mechanism or agentic power ensuring that the appropriate outcomes occur. Given actors are ruled out as the agents of history, what is the directing mechanism? The theorists were unclear. Parsons, for example, relies only on what has been called 'necessary reason'. For example, he explains the invention and continued existence of money by the fact that money makes resources mobile and the mobility of resources enhances survival capacity. But this sort of explanation is vacuous (Bershady 1973: 145–6). It amounts to saying that the problem somehow calls forth its solution! But how? The question for modernization theory and systems functionalism is w*hat* identifies problems and potential solutions, makes selections and investments? What is it that carries interests and strategically pursues them?

In fact Parsons adopts a teleological view of human history and societies. Teleology argues that the future pulls the present towards it and that history is a process with a design and destination. Parsons implies societies have the capacity to anticipate the consequences for their survival of social developments and that anticipation of the effects of what happens directs events. In other words, societies are credited with powers of agency. This contrasts strongly with the biological theory of evolution which avoids teleology because species changes which turn out to increase adaption to the environment are not intentional but the result of random mutation and environmental change. The theory can be used to explain change retrospectively, but also shows why we cannot know in advance what the species of the future will be like. In this sense it is fully historical.

Traditional social evolutionary thinking has often been criticized for taking biology as its model, on the grounds that social realities are not biological realities (Giddens 1984: 237). But its really serious mistake has been that it has missed what is specifically historical about the biological theory of evolutionary change. This shows us what any theory of unpredictable change must look like, even when the mechanisms are not biological ones. This is an issue we will return to in Part Three.

The critique of social integration: conflict, power and interests

There are two interrelated fronts along which to advance beyond the utopian vagueness and empirical implausibility of modernization theory and its notion of end-seeking systems (Dahrendorf 1958). The first is to develop ideas about how social systems contribute to their own formation and change. This requires conceptualizing social systems as having change-producing properties (but not pseudo-intentionality) and avoiding teleological assumptions. It involves being as specific as possible about the *systemic* sources of change. The fact that Parsons failed to specify these does not mean that there are none. However, specifying them will have to take the other front into account, which is to 'bring men back in' (Homans 1964) and establish the role of actors, both collective and individual, in the historical process, asking how intentional action contributes to producing change. This rehumanizing of social theory by focusing on action is dealt with in the next chapter. Here I need only point out that the recovery of human agency was central to the general critique of claims that the social world is unproblematically *integrated* (Lockwood 1966). This task followed from the late 1960s experience of malintegration when the political and cultural events contradicted modernization theory's account of good fit between the parts of social systems and normative consensus between people. That systems had strong compulsory powers, but often contradictory effects, and that there were deep conflicts of interest and an absence of consensus, became so obvious that modernization theory was increasingly ridiculed.

In fact the dominant critical response to normative functionalism was 'conflict theory' (Dahrendorf 1959, Rex 1961). This, as Lockwood so brilliantly showed, developed an alternative understanding of change by concentrating solely on *relations between people* – what he calls *social integration*. Change is produced because the relations between actors are conflictual, not consensual. Conflict theory postulates differences of interest and values which are related to differences of power. It 'brings men back in', avoids reification, and is certainly a major step away from the over-integrated picture of Parsonian functionalism. But as social theory, it is limited by its assumption that conflict always produces change (Lockwood 1966: 245–9). It replaces normative functionalism's one-sided commitment to system stability with an equally one-sided commitment to system change.

Lockwood's antidote was to distinguish between *social integration* (the relations between people) and *system integration* (the relations between parts of systems). The analysis of relations between the parts of systems was already the stock-in-trade of 'general functionalism' (represented by Merton (1957) and clearly distinguished from the 'normative' and 'systems' varieties!) and Marxism. Both analyse the effects of the way the parts of social systems are related to establish the extent of their integration. But neither assume functional integration. 'Dysfunction' is as possible as function. Whether there is 'good fit' has to be determined for every actual case. The defining concept is that of 'dysfunction', which is the equal of 'function'. Lockwood insisted that social and system integration are not only analytically separable but also, because each has its own temporality, factually distinguishable (1966: 250). So it becomes possible to deal with the two types of case not recognized by normative functionalism and conflict theory: that where social integration is high but system integration is low, making change likely, and that where social integration is low but system integration high, making change rather unlikely. Of course, change is most probable when both are low. In other words, a comprehensive theory of change must distinguish between relations between parts of systems and relations between people, and show how both these kinds of relations interact in specific cases. The existence of normative consensus, or its opposite, tells us very little about the prospects for change. What is needed is an analysis of the condition of the systems within which these relations between people occur – which was the immediate focus of the first front advancing beyond modernization theory.

The dialectical understanding of the mechanism of social systems

The problem of more adequately conceptualizing the change-producing character of social systems led straight to Marx and the dialectical tradition. Marx was attractive for many reasons but I shall only deal with those that were of fundamental importance for developing the understanding of structuration and 'structuration' theory. 'Structurationist' thought is an heir to the dialectical tradition. It is the dialectical element, directly opposing the notion of progressive integration, which is missing from modernization theory.

Marx, following Hegel, thinks there are two kinds of change which are related, change *in* systems (we might call this normal change) and change *of* systems (we might call this revolutionary change). The conditions for the reproduction of systems vary systematically over time. So, in the early phase of capitalism, the conditions for expanding it, increasing production using wage labour and making profit, are good. But by virtue of the very success of this expansion, there comes a time when limits set in, and there is a 'declining rate of profit'. What once worked well no longer does so. Thus, rather than the evolutionary utopia of a history of unceasing gains in efficiency, Marx theorizes the inevitable production by the system itself of the conditions of its own destruction. These conditions are the emergent 'negative' contradictions between system parts which were, at an earlier phase, functionally integrated. Marx's theory of systems incorporates the possibility that dysfunctional effects will emerge over time. The possibility of variable functionality among the parts of systems, the idea that dysfunctionality may be internally generated by systems themselves, and the idea that systems may be revolutionized into qualitatively new forms as a result, are the three elements which contradict modernization theory. Marx (anticipating Merton) helpfully offers the possibility that the relations between the parts of systems may be either integrative or disintegrative.

More problematic is Marx's assumption that the disintegration, change and reintegration of modes of production follows one predetermined pattern. This brings him close to social evolutionism and, as the next chapter shows, makes avoiding reification difficult. But his insights about systems could be developed in a less grandiose and deterministic fashion. For example, they suggest that there is always a problem of systems integration between the material conditions of production and the established institutions of production. So, for example, rigid hierarchies tend to be dysfunctional for achieving rapid innovation. Lockwood refers to Weber's analysis of the predicament of the bureaucracies of the ancient world. They needed to raise taxes to rule but, in a subsistence economy and lacking modern administrative techniques, had to use local elites to gather them. This increased the power of these elites who were encouraged to increase their independence from the bureaucracy. As Weber puts it, 'The ruler attempts to expropriate the estates, and the estates attempt to expropriate the ruler' (Weber 1967: 298). So in trying to preserve their strength, these bureaucracies systematically undermined themselves, though not necessarily catastrophically. What this sort of systems analysis does is identify the functional requirements and contradictions of systems, which constrain the activity and relations between people – rulers, bureaucrats, local strong men, priests, peasants and townsmen. How they relate to each other is shaped by the system-induced 'binds' they find themselves in. They cannot just get rid of the problems; they must deal with them in some way, by forming alliances of various kinds and by being more or less aggressive, compromising, deceitful, or whatever (Lockwood 1966: 253–4; Archer 1995: 222–5).

What this more modest, but nonetheless very important, form of systems analysis shows is that systems have objective and constraining properties which are vital for understanding change. But it makes no claim that these properties are sufficient to explain change. They are not the mechanisms of change suggested by systems functionalism and social evolutionism. Such analysis conceptualizes systems as incomplete; to have their effects there have to be people whose activity is constrained by them.

Recovering
Human Agency

History for the making

As we have seen in the previous chapter, normative functionalism and evolutionism had attempted to explain historical change and the structuration of society as a natural process, but without supplying the necessary mechanism. The result was an ahistorical utopia (Dahrendorf 1958). Systems are simply held to seek to differentiate while maintaining integration in order to survive. There are no sources of system transformation at work internally (Sjoberg 1960). Such theorizing could neither understand contemporary change, nor suggest what practical steps might be taken to steer its direction – given that this was predetermined. These failings motivated a search for theoretical resources with which to open up history. The search travelled along a broad front, scooping up anything which might contribute to undermining modernist evolutionary determinism, including alternative forms of determinism. However, rejecting 'Parsonian' systems theory simply cleared the field for the constructive task of providing a coherent replacement. I cannot detail all the elements that were then advanced as candidates to replace or contribute to the replacement of systems theory. But it is necessary to present a brief characterization of the main contenders because 'structuration' theory emerged from the dilemmas of the theoretical field they constituted.

Fragmentation and the tendency to polarization

In the last chapter we considered Lockwood's constructive response to Parsons and 'conflict theory'. He argued that explaining social change required reference to (a) the properties of objective social phenomena such as institutions and how they are interrelated (systems integration) (b) the properties of the interaction and activity of people (social integration) and (c) the relations between these two different constituents. This amounts to an elementary, but profound, account of structuration. Lockwood recognizes the need to distinguish between, and relate, social systems and actors. They are conditions of one another's existence and of the way they change (see Figure 1.1). We shall return to Lockwood's prescription repeatedly.

However, what came to be known as 'structuration' theorizing did not directly follow Lockwood's lead as it might have done. Rather it responded to the fragmentation of social theory consequent upon both the uncompromising opposition to Parsons and the equally strong hostility of some of his attackers to each other. To understand the emergence of 'structuration' theorizing it is now helpful to conceptualize this whole theoretical field as cross-cut by two major fissures. The first was between Marxism and bourgeois sociology (which included Parsons and some of his opponents), the second between objectivism (systems analysis, structural causation, and the social determinism associated with Parsons) and 'subjectivism' (action theory, voluntarism, interactionism, phenomenology). 'Structuration' theorizing followed on the heels of this combatative phase of emphatic contradiction, and began to sort out the genuine novelties from what now appeared as overstatement, building a synthesis of ideas drawn from both sides of these two divides. We can now consider each of the fissures in turn, though they are interlinked.

Marxism and 'bourgeois sociology'

Marxism was politically attractive because, as shown in the last chapter, it combined a robust conception of systemic sources of change with an insistence on human actors' contribution to making history. Its difficulty lay in specifying the exact relation between the two 'sides', which Marx himself regarded as part of one process. Theorists tended to assign priority to one or the other. Systems were *either reified* (denuded of genuine human agency) *or reduced* by being made effects of voluntary action by class subjects. The result was the tendency of Marxism to divide into an objectivist 'scientific' wing and a subjectivist, 'humanist' or 'critical' wing (Gouldner 1980).

For objectivists, Marxism's concept of social systems and powerful account of the systemic mechanism of change, employing the concept of structural contradiction, offered a platform for securing scientific status. Change emanated from within systems. Those who thought in this way produced 'scientific' or 'structuralist' Marxism, varying in the extent to which they emphasized economic causation, or the interaction of economic and non-economic causes (Benton 1984). Where causal plurality was stressed, their Marxism took on properties of normative functionalism (Lockwood 1981: 76). Institutions and practices became functionally interdependent, cohered by the integrating effects of 'ideology' (DiTomaso 1982). Incorporating non-economic factors into the account of systems also weakened the capacity to identify specific levers of change – what had originally made Marxism attractive. Structuralist Marxists were 'anti-humanist'; just as in Parsons's functionalism, human actors or 'subjects' were theorized as social material which had to be formed to perform its social functions. There is little space between Parsons's 'socialization' and Althusser's 'ideological interpolation'. Both evolutionary functionalism and structuralist Marxism fail to solve the problem of how to incorporate the human material into the theory of history. To insist on the necessity for controlling and integrating mechanisms is to admit the existence of entities, call them human beings, which pre-exist their socialization. Though socialization may be necessary for humans to become subjects capable of self-directing action, it is not sufficient. Social theoretical structuralism, of whatever stripe, must postulate the potential for subjectivity which its anti-humanism inclines it to deny (Clarke 1981: 210–35; Anderson 1983: 32–55; Soper 1986: 96–119; Burkitt 1991).

Marxist structuralism was as guilty as systems functionalism of reification. It failed to fulfil the promise of reopening history which the idea of systems contradiction offered. Marx's great contribution, recognized by Lockwood, was to provide a systems analysis which *recognized objective systemic sources of change whilst avoiding reification*. 'Structuration' theorists and their critics eventually followed this example, retaining Marx's humanist side, revealed in his early critiques of reification and alienation popularized through new translations and collections in the 1960s (e.g. Bottomore and Rubel 1961; Marx [1857–8]1964, [1857–8]1973;

Marx and Engels [1846]1965). The objects of Marx's 'science of history' were populated by 'real' human beings with a full set of generic and universal species characteristics. It was this which seemed most immediately relevant for opening up history. Marx's account of structuration demanded a specification of the properties of human actors which were relevant for his 'science of history'.

Marx's influence on the problem of historical agency is difficult to overstate. The early writings provide a sustained systematic critique of philosophical anthropology (Avineri 1968; Ollman 1971; Hughes *et al.* 1995). Marx's human beings are social animals in a practical relation with the material world. Uniquely this species engages its environment practically through its consciousness and imagination. Humans have actively to produce the necessities of life by labouring to transform what nature provides. In this sense, they creatively produce their own conditions of life. Hence the large variety of ways of life the historical record reveals. Marx rebuts idealism and 'vulgar' materialism. As the *Eleven Theses on Feuerbach* concisely shows, humans are not active 'subjects' just because they can think and, though they are material beings, they do not simply react to environmental stimuli with their genetic endowment. Human subjectivity asserted by idealism is combined with the objectivity claimed by materialism. Moreover, Marx rejects attempts to specify human nature by referring to discrete individuals. 'The real nature of man is the totality of social relations' (Thesis 6), meaning that individuals are always socially related and that these relations confer productive powers on them (Bottomore and Rubel 1961: 83). The dualism (i.e. separation) of individuals and society is dismissed, as is any attempt to derive social properties (for example market behaviour) from pre-social properties of individuals. Marx thinks of human beings as creative, because they are social subjects – the 'history-producing' species.

Humanist Marxism offers a mode of theorizing the relation between structure and agency which has strengths but also major weaknesses. These make it difficult for it to specify the history-producing capacity of particular agents in specific structural conditions – for example the historical agency of the working class under capitalism. Marxism argues that modes of production ('structure' or systems) differentiate and collectivize people into systematically opposed classes. These 'locations' condition agency by defining the objective interests of each class. It uses this structural conditioning of interests to link structure to agency. Marxism, in

Parsons's terms, 'de-randomizes' ends and contributes to the rejection of utilitarian individualism by suggesting that structure determines interests and interests determine ends.

It cannot be stressed too much that offering a social-structural account of 'interests' and 'ends' is fundamental to the 'structurationist' project. The 'structure' side of things has to impact on the formation of ends, if individualism is to be avoided (Bauman 1989). However, in the case of the Marxist theory of agency, class structure has been insufficient to explain the variety of ends which are actually sought. It can't explain why the western working class, theorized as having an objective interest in revolutionizing capitalism, has not done so (Lockwood 1966; 1981; Mann 1973). It has failed because of the poverty of its understanding of the way people relate to each other, that is how they are socially integrated. Marxism generally only recognizes one way of relating to others, that is on the basis of class location and the rational calculation (technical and economic) of the best means of furthering class interest. Individuals and organizations are treated as class agents, orientating to their situation in purely cognitive and rational terms. So the theory is still rooted in utilitarianism. Instead of rational, self-seeking individuals with random ends, Marx offers rational, self-seeking classes with system-induced ends.

This is a very limited view of human actors and their potential for historical agency. It restricts the kind of ends they seek to one – those determined by their objective economic interests, and the criteria for choosing means to one – that is, the rational. Faced with the facts, that the proletariat has not done what the theory suggests it should, Marxism has to explain how the objective interests are not recognized or do not lead to the expected choice of ends. It does this by proposing 'ideological' mechanisms which make the working class ignorant or irrational. These defences imply that workers are culturally determined. So we have a theory which regards class actors as voluntary historical subjects, but only when they are rational; and when they are not, as involuntary objects of forces beyond their control. Given the abundance of 'irrationality' in the history of the capitalist working class, Marxism has little choice but to explain most of that history in deterministic terms. This puts its basic ontological commitment to the possibility of historical agency on the line.

The problem is that Marxism's theory of action is too restrictive in what it recognizes as conferring agency on actors. The 'rationality/objective interests' model means that very little of what people do can be regarded as voluntary action. The remedy, so carefully specified by Lockwood using Parsons, is to widen the criteria actors use to orient action, to include the 'normative'. This refers to the realm of values which are not explicable in terms of cognition and means–ends calculative rationality. They constitute the 'non-rational' rather than the 'irrational' (Parsons: [1937]1968: 712–13; Lockwood 1981: 62). For Marxism, to admit the force of 'non-rational' sources of interest is to step warily into the province of 'bourgeois sociology', putting its identity as a separate tradition, let alone a 'science', at risk.

The Durkheimian and Weberian traditions offer much more complex accounts of actors, action and social integration. They recognize that human actors have ideas about how they should act and what should be the case – they have 'ideals'. One cannot identify how to act simply on the basis of empirical knowledge about a situation and the most rational way to use the available means to a given end. Actors must choose using values that specify what is *desirable*. Durkheim and Weber converge on the idea that action involves both practical, and ideal, considerations. It therefore has 'a doubly normative orientation . . . to efficiency norms and to legitimacy norms' (Parsons [1937]1968: 710). The way people relate to one another is therefore mediated by ideas about what is desirable and right. These ideas and values are institutionalized into cultural traditions and provide a major element of socialization. In this light the 'non-rational' element in action is the response to a sense of obligation to uphold some value as an end in itself. Action is as grounded by moral values as it is by economic interest. Bourgeois sociology focuses on the sources of these values, how they develop and change in relation to material circumstances, how they are reproduced, institutionalized and internalized, and acquire a measure of autonomy. The cultural relations which flow from the 'non-rational' are as fundamental as 'relations of production'. They are just as 'objective' and 'systematic', and just as much a product of the creative action of human beings.

When directed to the question of the historical agency of the working class, this frame of reference explains class action by referring to the cultural processes leading to the formation of 'ideals' for life, the sense of obligation to others and what is right – the moral fabric with its often contradictory pressures. These processes work at the level of the experience of specific circumstances and contexts of interaction. From this perspective, Marx's working class appears to be internally differentiated, hierarchicized, and able to produce its own cultural traditions which are not merely under-standings of 'objective' economic interests, nor determined by some 'dominant ideology' (Abercrombie *et al.* 1980). In other words, workers are not 'socially integrated' by virtue of their class relations and have other than intrasystemic interests. They are situated in concrete contexts of interaction, with their regional, occupational and historical distinctiveness. They possess different historical and cultural legacies with which to respond to the experi-ence of class relations. In fact, this is the sort of picture which emerges from the empirical work of the great Marxist historians, most notably E. P. Thompson (1963), and from the tradition of community studies and the empirical studies of various sub-categories of the working class, most notably *The Affluent Worker* (Goldthorpe, Lockwood *et al.* 1968–9).

From this standpoint 'systems integration' includes relations between the parts of culture, as well as institutional and economic relations, and 'social integration' refers to the effect of moral status on relations between people. The picture of moral beings orient-ing their action in terms of norms means that social integration cannot be reduced to systems integration. It increases actors' scope for historical agency because they are no longer limited to uncom-promising rationality. This recovery of the moral dimension of human social relations motivated the 1960s revival of interest in the classical sociologists and, ironically, the early Parsons, whose *The Structure of Social Action* was published in paperback in 1968 ([1937]1968). Giddens himself was an important contributor to this recovery with his best-selling *Capitalism and Modern Social Theory* (1971).

Objectivism, reification and subjectivism

The dominant tendency in the development of social theory prior to the 'structurationist' moment was opposition to Marxist and non-Marxist versions of reifying objectivism. Normative functionalism, modernization theory and structuralist Marxism tried to account for historical change as an effect of the objective self-moving powers of systems. Relations between system elements explain everything. People occupying positions and roles created by systems lack powers to affect them. They act executively but not voluntarily or creatively, are 'objects' not 'subjects'. But given the failure of reified social theory to account for empirical historical development (modernization produces imperialist barbarism, the proletariat fails to produce the revolution), there are not simply moral, but also good intellectual grounds, to reintroduce a conceptualization of people as historically effective actors, that is agents. Hence the late sixties interest in those approaches to history based on the subjectivity of people. The early Marx, German historicism, French existentialism, Durkheim's 'science of moral life', and especially Weber's interpretative sociology of action were all employed to get subjectivity back into the frame.

Lockwood's critique of the Marxist theory of class action discussed in Chapter 2 showed some of what Durkheim and Weber have to offer. They see people positioned within social systems with objective properties, relating to each other in terms of culturally given criteria, used, for example, to determine social status. People act and interact on the basis of the subjective meaning of the elements of social situations which they determine by interpreting them. This interpreting of situations to establish their meaning is a lot more complicated than utilitarianism suggests.

This complexity was addressed in two ways. First, the objective properties of cultural systems and language were investigated in more or less reified ways. Those drawing on the hermeneutic tradition saw cultural 'stuff' as a resource which people use, requiring interpretation by them to become meaningful. At the other reifying extreme, for French structuralist anthropologists, cultural systems determined meaning objectively, constraining actors with some inescapable logic. Second, and by far the most significant for the development of any form of structuration theory, was *the investigation of the subjectivity of actors and of action itself.* This built on the critique of utilitarianism suggesting actors are more than individual rational calculators. They are *socially related,* have *social identities* from which flow *moral obligations* and commitments to *values* of various kinds. The investigation of subjectivity centred on what is involved in 'orienting' to action situations, the process of interpretation, and the elaboration of what 'rationality' itself means. I will discuss each briefly.

Weber and Durkheim, champions of the 'non-rational', showed that orienting to action situations is a matter of articulating knowledge, rationality, self-conscious commitments to values, and unreflexive emotional preferences. Individuals are not necessarily aware of their deeper motives. Much action is routine, explicable by reference to what is expected by or acceptable to a cultural community. The rational assessment of means is not the most general case. Emotion and conforming to tradition explain far more. The exploration of subjectivity took off from these insights to analyse the nature of 'everyday life' and what makes it possible to act without the kind of rational deliberation envisaged by utilitarianism. Of major importance was Schutz's existential social phenomenology (Schutz [1932]1967, 1964–67; Giddens 1976: 24–33). This analysed how it was possible for individuals to live with a secure sense of reality – 'the natural attitude'. Schutz's social phenomenology explained why the world was not fundamentally problematic. It is doubt, not belief, which is suspended by 'common sense', whose rationality actors use to orient to situations. This form of rationality is essentially practical, consisting of 'procedures' for maintaining meaningfulness in the midst of the muddle and uncertainty of 'lived-through experience'. Meaning is tentative, provisional, changing as time passes, so that retrospection becomes as important as the 'prospective deliberation' implicit in the utilitarian model of rationality.

For Schutz, all individuals construct social reality for themselves, using cultural 'typifications' and 'recipes' to interpret their experience of others. His claim that a meaning-endowing 'ego-consciousness' constitutes the social world provides an extreme case of the tendency of focusing on subjectivity to end up removing social reality entirely from the realm of objects (Schutz [1932]1967: 37). Ethnomethodologists, particularly Garfinkel, developed the analysis of the methods of common sense, turning away from the mental life of individuals to focus on how people make events publicly 'accountable' and meaningful 'for the time being' (Garfinkel 1967). Here, though 'social order' is still treated as only a 'representation' of order, an objective element is retained by making the process of constructing such representations a matter of achieving justification in practical contexts of interaction. Garfinkel explores what is involved in being 'reasonable' for members of communities as they deal with the contingencies of life, keeping things going. This involves 'ethnomethods' for applying or suspending rules (defining what ought to happen) to actual events. Rationality is a practical business of articulating the reality with public ideals. Where the rules (ideals) cannot be adhered to, they are upheld by excusing, ignoring and forgiving in the light of 'what everybody knows' are the difficulties (Zimmerman 1971: 227). Rationality is essentially practical, public and moral – in a word, socially integrating – and a far cry from utilitarianism.

Ethnomethodology has the great merit of situating the operation of subjectivity in the immediacy of concrete contexts of interaction and practical activity. It emphasizes the common experience of the details of such contexts which are used to ground the reasonableness of the descriptions and justifications actors construct. But this 'context-dependence' is similar to Schutz's 'mind-dependence', in that it reduces the reality of social structures to their imaginary existence for subjects, individually (Schutz) or collectively (Garfinkel). The focus is so concentrated on the agency and context of producing meaning that the reference of social structure has been reduced to representations of it, with the duration of the contexts in which the subjects do the representing. Reification is certainly avoided but at the price of the reduction of social structure to the level of persons and interaction. The door begins to close on the wider extra-situational context and on the reality of historical structures. Neither biographical time, nor the relatively short duration of practical contexts or episodes of interaction, can sustain the extended duration required to conceptualize history. The time frame contracts towards the immediacy of interaction.

Schutz and Garfinkel exemplify how enthusiasm for the powers of subjectivity, motivated by a 'rage for agency' against reified social theory, so easily overshoots the mark to verge on uncompromising subjectiv*ism*. Instead of reification, where agents are effects of social systems, we get *reduction*, where social systems are effects of agents. Determinism/objectivism and voluntarism/subjectivism polarize. Dawe made this clear in his 'The two sociologies' (1970) where he summarized the contemporary sense of the irreconcilable differences between a 'sociology of systems' and a 'sociology of action', arguing that these were matters of doctrine and the utopian values of the sociologist. He favoured the sociology of action and the explanation of behaviour in terms of the 'central meanings' of actors. Typically he cites the *Affluent Worker* studies as investigations of the 'consciousness' of workers, rather than of the relation between their terms of social integration and their position in the class structure as the authors intended.

However, there is another option besides objectivist 'reification' or subjectivist 'reduction', and that is to incorporate both objectivity and subjectivity in the conceptualizing of social reality and

change. This is the relational option. We have already seen Lockwood mobilize one version of it where he distinguishes but then
relates social and system integration. The relational position does
not envisage some perfect integration in terms of either objects or
subjects, but seeks in various ways to relate apparently irreconcilable elements.

Arriving on the theoretical scene which I have been mapping out
in this and the preceding chapter, those treading the 'structurationist' path tried to capitalize on the recovery of agency, stopping
well short of subjectivism, whilst simultaneously maintaining a
healthy respect for the constraining powers of structure without
succumbing to outright objectivism. As we shall see in the next two
chapters, they also saw the problem of relating structure and agency
as an ontological one – that is, as a problem of how social reality
in general should be understood. Approached like this, they felt
the solution required reconceptualizing structure and agency so as
to remove any contradiction between them, unifying them in a
relation of logically necessary interdependence. That is, they felt
that structure and agency constituted a 'duality'.

However, there was another possible way of avoiding subject-
ivism and object*ivism* and linking structure and agency already pre-
figured in Lockwood's work. It involved suggesting that relating of
structure and agency must recognize that each involves relations of
quite different kinds and that *interaction of these two kinds of
relations* is a matter for empirical historical analysis case by case,
since the relation between system elements and social elements is
historically emergent. Such an historical approach maintains the
dualism of objective system elements and the voluntary agency of
human subjects. It is this necessity of recognizing both the *inter-
relatedness* and the *distinction between* subject and object which is
reasserted by the post-'structurationist' theories discussed in Part
Three.

PART TWO

The 'Structurationists'

4

Bourdieu: Structuration through Power

Introduction

This chapter and the next describe the different ways Bourdieu and Giddens follow the 'structurationist' path. Rather than comprehensively rehearsing their work I concentrate on (a) how they specify the problem of accounting for structure and agency, and (b) their respective conceptual innovations designed to solve it.

Bourdieu prefers 'genetic structuralism' to 'structuration' theory to describe his work (Bourdieu 1990: 14). But he is widely, and I think correctly, held to have tackled essentially the same fundamental problems of social theory as Giddens – and earlier (Lash 1990: 254; May 1996: 120; Baert 1998: 32). In fact I suggest he exempifies 'structurationist' thinking and was (and is) in tune with the demand for it. Despite his hostility to Giddens's mode of producing theory (which he dubs 'theoretical theory' or 'scholastic'), he cannot easily avoid being associated with Giddens's ideas (Bourdieu and Wacquant 1992: 3).

Interestingly, both authors make very limited reference to each other's work. Giddens refers approvingly to Bourdieu's critique of Levi-Strauss's analysis of the gift (Giddens 1979: 25–6); briefly discusses 'habitus', interpreting it to mean 'habits' (Giddens 1979: 217); cites Bourdieu's discussion of time reckoning in Kabylia (Giddens 1984: 133), and the notion of cultural capital in a critique of Gouldner (Giddens 1987: 273). There is a review of *Distinction* (Giddens 1986: 300–5). This hardly constitutes an adequate or systematic engagement with ideas that precede and parallel his own. Conversely, one might have expected Bourdieu to have responded to Giddens's work by now, if only with the kind of splenetic remarks he has directed at unsympathetic critics (Bourdieu and Waquant 1992: 169). But I do not think this has happened. Perhaps, besides his disapproval of developing theory distanced from empirical research, Bourdieu senses in Giddens more ally than foe. Be this as it may, interpreting Bourdieu in the light of 'structuration', and developing the comparison with Giddens more systematically than is usually done, is a way of revealing the generic properties of 'structurationist' reasoning despite the considerable differences in the styles in which it has been pursued.

Experience and theory

One effective way of introducing Bourdieu is to focus on the concept of 'experience' and its role in knowledge production. Fundamental to his thinking is the idea that human existence is embodied. Living through our bodies positions each of us to experience the world immediately and uniquely. We are equipped to register qualities and changes in the world, a registering variously described as 'being aware', 'sensing', 'feeling', 'intuiting'. Such experience 'flows' endlessly, and is the object of efforts to represent it using some language to communicate its social relevance. The result is some sort of knowledge. For Bourdieu, and the phenomenological and pragmatic traditions he draws upon, human being is characterized by this dialectical relation between the givenness of experience, and language; between the prepredicative, the prediscursive and prereflective, on the one hand, and the discursive and reflective on the other (May 1996: 36, 127). Bourdieu's interest in Husserl, Heidegger, Merleau-Ponty, Wittgenstein, Schutz, even Durkheim, and latterly Dewey, is motivated by what they reveal about what precedes and underpins language, rational reflection and argument (Bourdieu and Waquant 1992: 122). Their message is anti-intellectualist and anti-dualist. Mind, reflective consciousness, subjectivity, are dialectically interdependent with the body, prereflective experience and objectivity.

Bourdieu's approach to social theory has been forged by the need to use it to make sense of a certain kind of empirical experience, that is ethnographic experience. He tellingly describes informants as talking to the ethnologist as they would to a child, someone who knows nothing and has to have everything made explicit in the form of rules and lessons (Bourdieu 1986: 112). But helpful though such formulae may be, they provide us with a rather artificially reflective kind of knowledge. What we ought to be after, according to Bourdieu, is the knowledge of people who do not need to have things spelled out, the kind of knowledge that underpins the formulation of rules and the instructing of children/ethnologists. And what precedes the formulation of rules, instructions and what can be called theory is practice. The phenomenological emphasis on the priority of experience is coupled to the pragmatic and Marxist emphasis on the priority of practice. Ours is not merely embodied being, but doing.

Practice, practices, time and history: accounting for history in terms of practice

Bourdieu several times refers to Marx's *Eleven Theses on Feuerbach* as expressing the concept of practice which he seeks to recover and place at the foundation of sociology (Bourdieu 1985: 13; Bourdieu and Waquant 1992: 121). He wants to rescue 'the active side' from idealism, meaning that humans do not simply interpret their experience of the world, but actively produce it. 'Consciousness' does not contemplate the world from some separate vantage point, but encounters it as the practical concern of an embodied actor who is located at a position in time and space. Practice is only a spectacle to non-participants such as incompetents and visiting ethnologists (Bourdieu [1972]1977: 1–2).

His empirical studies of Kabylia, Bearn, kinship, religion, arts consumption, fashion, sport, photography and academic life all show individuals engaged in practices, doing things in patterned but not wholly identical ways. Individuals are seen to act in typical ways which are, to an important degree, predictable. They seem to have little difficulty in knowing what has to be done or how to do it, consulting rules only when they get stuck or have to explain themselves to non-participants. Whatever is constraining them to keep within the patterns of a way of life seems to sit lightly on them. Bourdieu's ethnographic experience suggests that it is unhelpful to conceptualize individuals as other than socially formed and fully engaged in social worlds. The individual and the social are not mutually exclusive categories. Individuals must therefore be regarded as collective beings and one basic task of social theory is to say how the patterning of individuals, and what they do, happens.

But equally, explanations of patterning must also explain the impressive variability and uniqueness which marks each instance or episode of practice. Bourdieu sees this element of indeterminacy arising from two conditions: first, irreducible differences between actors, and second, variations between the historical circumstances in which practice is conducted. It is these two kinds of difference which make it impossible for sociological generality to be more than typicality. Episodes of practice are necessarily historically unique. They involve using the capacity (skill) to undertake activity which will count as an instance of pursuing a particular practice, but by creatively operationalizing, interpreting and transforming elements in the context of action and bending them to the pursuit of the practice. Practice is the application of 'embodied understanding' to determine the relevance of general principles such as rules, recipes, formal procedures, judgemental criteria of all sorts, to specific cases (Taylor 1993). It is what is done to act here and now in response to what Bourdieu calls 'the urgency of practice' (Bourdieu [1980]1990: 82, 1990: 112). Useful social theory, theory which avoids the 'scholastic fallacy', has to give absolute priority to practice, the cutting edge of human existence (Bourdieu 1981: 310). It is practice which relates all the elements referred to by the traditional dichotomies: individual, society; material, ideal; mind, body; subject, object; being and becoming.

The reference to the concept of 'becoming' is crucial because it focuses attention on practice as relating moments of time and levels of history. What is cut at the cutting edge is the future. Through practice we 'become'; there is no standing still, we have to get on with it! Practice takes time. It relates past, present and future, to bring some future into being. 'Practice unfolds in time . . . Its temporal structure, that is its rhythm, its tempo, and above all its directionality, is constitutive of its meaning . . . Practice is inseparable from temporality' (Bourdieu [1980]1990: 81). However, this temporality is multi-layered; there is the immediacy of moments of practice, exemplified by bits of skilful play during a game such as tennis, the longer term level of projects which require a more extended sense of 'what one is doing' and, at the most extended level, the production and transformation of those practices and institutions which are historical in the sense of persisting longer than particular individuals or projects, and serving to frame the activity of individuals. Though talking as if there were only three levels of the temporality of practice is crude, it helps make the point that Bourdieu sees a continuous influence in both directions, between the most immediate and the most historically extended levels of temporality. Each is a condition of the other. So what the skilful tennis player does at a moment during a particular game may be of the utmost significance for all the higher levels of practice; games, careers, coaching, competitions, tennis, sports, leisure, class, economy. Economy, class, leisure etc. also impact on the particular game. The practice of individuals needs historically formed practices and vice versa: present practice is framed by history and the historical frames are made in the present.

For Bourdieu, practice is the key to historical understanding. It provides a position from which to attack any suggestion that history can be understood by prioritizing only one or a few of the elements referred to by the traditional dichotomies. Only practice satisfies his requirement that understanding must be relational, and subverts 'the rock-bottom antinomy upon which all the divisions of the social scientific field are ultimately founded, namely, the opposition between objectivism and subjectivism' (Bourdieu 1988: 780).

Positions and dispositions; accounting for practice

Bourdieu claims that the scientific use of theory requires 'actively reproduc(ing) the best products of past thinkers' in a spirit of 'humility' (Bourdieu 1985: 14–15). There is complete symmetry between his account of practice – what we study, and his account of method – how we study. We apply the tools of science to new objects and in new contexts and develop the tools as we go along. Bourdieu's contribution to a social theory centred on practice is to try to answer the question, 'what must be the entities and processes which result in the combination of determination and freedom, the predictable patterns and the unpredictable innovation and historical novelties, which characterize the social world revealed by ethnographic experience and history?' What, in other words, makes practice possible? This is where his modest claim to conceptual originality lies. The category of practice may specify a theoretical possibility for avoiding the traditional options, but it has to be given some detailed theoretical specification.

Bourdieu answers his question, and moves to give the detail, by concentrating on what actors need to engage in practice of any sort.

How can they interpret their experiences and cope with the 'urgency of practice'? His answer is that there is a dialectic of 'position and disposition', for which he recovers the medieval scholastics' term 'habitus', itself an interpretation of the Aristotelian term, 'hexis' (Bourdieu 1985: 12–13). Being practical requires actors to relate to the particularity of situations, size them up fast, evaluate them from some point of view, and know what to do – just like a games player. Fundamental to the idea of habitus is that individual actors are located within social groups (Weber) and classes (Weber and Marx) which compete to maintain and improve their standing in various 'fields' in which kinds of 'capital' are at stake. Both the competing collectivities and the fields over which they compete are historically produced structures. An historically significant collectivity is one capable of reproducing itself, that is, sustaining the pursuit of a typical set of interests, and inculcating in individuals a durable disposition which is transposable between fields, enabling them to engage in practice from the collectivity's point of view. This disposition or habitus is the mark of individuals who have been formed into typical examples of their group or class, and are thereby equipped with a way of relating to themselves (an identity) and the situations they encounter, without a second thought. Bourdieu socializes prereflexivity (influenced by Durkheim) and makes it into the generative principle of practice (influenced by structuralism). Though habitus, the 'strategy generating principle', is a universal of human practical agency, the content is plural and socially relative to formations capable of the long-term pursuit of their interests.

Equipped with a habitus – the concrete, embodied, interest-laden disposition which flows from being formed in a position, individuals become historical actors. By virtue of being given some historical and social specificity, they acquire the capacity to generate the creative, inventive pursuit of interests that is strategic practice. 'Every historical action brings together two states of history: objective history i.e. the history which has accumulated over the passage of time in things, . . . theories, customs, law etc.; and embodied history, in the form of habitus.' Habitus 'makes it possible to appropriate the legacy of history' (Bourdieu 1981: 305). 'Objectified history' becomes 'enacted history' when 'it is taken in charge by agents whose own history predisposes them to do so' and who have 'appropriate attributes to make it function . . . When the same history inhabits both habitus and habitat, both disposition and position . . .

History as "subject" discovers itself in history as "object" ' (Bourdieu 1981: 306). It is the creative use of a history in the practice of agents which keeps it 'alive' and moving on into the future.

Creativity, strategy, reproduction and transformation

Thus far we have the basis of Bourdieu's arguments against subjectivism and objectivism. Subjectivism's postulate of universal, creative, rational, calculating, self-directing and self-interested individuals is rejected. Instead, powers of agency accrue from being 'positioned' and socialized within historical structures of competing interests. Objectivism's postulate of mechanisms which function more or less automatically to sustain historical structures is rejected in favour of the view that they only persist because agents know how to apply them practically in ever-changing situations. The mechanism of Bourdieu's genetic structuralism is historical agency, or 'habitus-practice', and there is nothing automatic about its outcomes. Agency is constrained or restricted to some degree by its dependence upon being positioned, and is to that extent objectified. By the same token, the persistence of historical structures is made vulnerable to agents' creative use of them, and to that extent they are subjectified. Clearly Bourdieu has taken a path close to that of Lockwood but, by attacking the dualism of subject and object, is arguably nearer to Giddens (Figure 1.1).

We can now try to evaluate Bourdieu's way of relating agency and structure, and accounting for history. He refuses to oppose subjects and objects, but what is the status of his way of theorizing their mutual interdependence and how does it affect how they themselves are conceptualized? We can begin with agency and Bourdieu's analysis of how it is enabled and constrained. Creative agency is enabled, but constrained by habitus. What is enabled is a capacity to pursue interests as a typical example of a classed and grouped individual. The powers of agents have to begin somewhere if subjectivism is to be avoided. Agents are therefore, at minimum, constrained by their starting points. But accepting this rather banal truth tells us little about the possibilities for how agents might apply, change or relate to their starting points. We are all, in a weak sense, prisoners of the past. But this is quite compatible with claiming extensive powers of agency close to those postulated by subjectivism. However, Bourdieu thinks agents are also constrained by the 'urgency of practice' (reflective, rational deliberation about alternatives is a luxury) and by their position in the structure of advantage and disadvantage of ongoing struggles in the various fields (agents vary in their capacity to exercise power). Agents, in being constituted as agents, are also caught up in existing struggles and involuntarily committed to participating and taking sides. They are therefore constrained to seek certain ends. Agency extends to being a strategic competitor directing one's agency to supporting the interests of one's collectivity as it fights its corner in the various fields. The result is a dominant tendency in human life for agents to exercise their powers in ways which broadly tend to conserve a structure of competing groups and classes. People must become embroiled in social struggles, but are left considerable powers of agency, particularly over their choice and skilful deployment of the means of struggle. These powers, however, are less extensive than those asserted by subjectivism, because the 'autonomy of interest' – the core of subjectivism – has been given over to the objective side.

In addition, agents' power to determine the means of securing their interests is constrained by their relative advantage or disadvantage in the distribution of power within the fields of competition. Much of the plausibility of Bourdieu's conceptualization of the role of habitus derives from its being developed to explain the predictability of the behaviour of people inhabiting strongly institutionalized power structures. The traditional worlds of Kabylia and Bearn, as well as the workings of modern education systems, are characterized by effective long-term domination. They are historical products of long processes of struggle in which the dominant have consolidated their hold of advantage and instituted mechanisms (e.g. inheritance rules, marriage practices, status symbolism, 'meritocratic' examinations etc.) of 'symbolic violence' (Bourdieu [1972]1977: 183–97). The historical process has been long enough for the dominated and the dominant to have developed their respective cultures, which contain the accumulated expectations, presumptions, techniques and defences which have been found to work for them. The dominant have learned how to maintain their advantage and the dominated have learned how to defend the little they have in the way of possessions and self-respect. Where the exercise of power has become naturalized and routinized in symbolic form, with its characteristic 'euphemization', Bourdieu's picture of habitus as durable, transposable and overwhelmingly reproductive in its effects is at its most plausible. Here is the empirical support for his claim that there is 'ontological complicity' between agents and structures, as the dominated and the dominant routinely reproduce the structure and their respective locations within it. It is in historical conditions like this that it is plausible to suggest that agents 'anticipate' and 'adjust' their aspirations to likely outcomes and the 'immanent necessity' of situations, and that the dominated routinely contribute to their own domination. Bourdieu asks, 'Why, then, do agents "do the only thing that is to be done" more often than chance would predict?', and answers, 'Because they practically anticipate the immanent necessity of their social world, by following the intuitions of a practical sense that is the product of *a lasting subjection to conditions similar to the ones they are placed in*' (my emphasis) (Bourdieu 1988: 783).

Though the 'model of the near-circular relation of near-perfect reproduction' may be valid for the kinds of empirical cases which Bourdieu drew on to develop his theory, they are not the only ones (Bourdieu 1990: 63; Bourdieu and Waquant 1992: 130–1). Habitus may be a universal requirement of practice, but whether or not it takes a highly functional form in any setting depends on the particular historical process of establishing long-term relations of domination. Practice requires agents to use their habitus, a way of making sense which is the fruit of past experience, to give sense and value to their current experience, or in other terms, to identify ends and means. 'Lasting subjection' produces current experience sufficiently similar to past experience to confirm the terms of habitus, inhibit critical reflection about how things could be otherwise and routinize the choice of means. These will tend to be 'submissive'. This 'practical recognition of legitimacy' is expressed 'in the silence of shyness, abstention or resignation, by which the dominated manifest . . . their practical acceptance of the possibilities and the impossibilities inscribed in the field' (Bourdieu 1990: 112). Bourdieu is rather realistic – some might say pessimistic – about the limited (though never entirely absent) opportunities for the dominated to break out of their subjection. But the point here is that there is nothing inherently functionalist about the relation between habitus-practice and structure. The variable and historically contingent functionality of habitus is not functionalism (Bourdieu and Waquant 1992: 79–82; Jenkins 1992: 81–2). What must be remembered is that the various habituses are developed collectively by generations of people in response to the experience of

tending to win or lose as competitors in fields. Contexts where
habitus seems to be most functional for reproduction should be
regarded as relatively enduring moments in a longer history of the
institutionalizing of domination. Though, once instituted, the dominated may find it very difficult to change the order of things, it is
not the case that history somehow stops.

We can see from this that agency and structure are related by
power which has systematic effects on the way each is conceptualized. Thus structure confers agency on agents by distributing power
to them. Structures are distributional orders. Agents, as benefici-
aries of these orders, use their power to defend or increase their
holding, causing realignments within the distributional structure,
changes in habitus and innovation of, and within, fields. Agents are
thought of as desiring the power conferred by Bourdieu's four types
of capital – economic, political, social and cultural (symbolic). They
struggle for recognition as superior in every form of practice or
field (Cohen 1996: 138–9). Humans exist in a condition of what
Boyne (1993: 249) calls 'Machiavellian collectivity'. The principle
of historical action is struggle for advantage in fields. Historical
agency is conferred, not on the individual and rational subject of
subjectivism, but on collective agents constituted by their relations
of antagonism and domination. All that remains of the individual
as subject is its identity as a social self, oriented to certain interests, motivated to compete and pursue strategies to enhance its
power. With this disenchanting reduction, sociology frees us 'from
the misplaced belief in illusory freedoms' (Bourdieu 1990: 15;
McLennan 1998: 88). The subjectivity of actors is only rendered
'agentic' when collectivized by field struggles.

This 'relative devaluation of the subjective moment' (Fowler
1997: 5), with its cognitive and motivational straightforwardness,
should not be mistaken for a bias towards structural determination.
The devaluation is a symptom of the attempt to use power as the
substance of which agency and structure are aspects or forms.
Structure is similarly devalued by construing every kind of social
differentiation as the product of struggles for power. The possibility
of distinguishing *between* structures in terms of what causes their
internal differentiation is ruled out. And recognition of 'horizontal'
internal differentiation becomes problematic, given the intrinsic
connection between power struggles and stratifying effects. Non-
hierarchized occupational specialization triggered by technical
innovation, for example, becomes difficult to deal with. It seems

Bourdieu's anti-dualist argument that agency and structure are mutually implicated by power requires both be trimmed to suit. Agents must be reduced to power seekers and wielders, structures to hierarchies produced by power struggles. I suggest some form of trimming of agency and structure typifies *all* 'structurationist' efforts to establish their identity.

The limitations of deriving so much from power as a means of uniting structure and agency can be elaborated by reconsidering what is involved in practice within fields. For Bourdieu, practice requires embodied agents who experience situations, use the language and values of their 'practical sense' to make strategic judgements and, when that fails, to innovate on the basis of rational reflection. This general picture holds for all the different kinds of practices and their 'capitals' which support fields. The four elements of (a) embodied experience, (b) language and rationality, (c) values, and (d) the variety of practices are all implicated in the constitution of agency and structure. However, each can be argued to be *relatively autonomous*, capable of exercising a constituting effect prior to the distribution and struggles of power which fascinate Bourdieu. Maybe he puts the cart before the horse.

Consider language. It is used in all practices. Bourdieu claims that 'authority comes to language from outside', that is from the social position and 'delegated' authority of the speaker. This is partially true, but language also has 'internal' force by virtue of the logic of statements for which truth is claimed. Powerful or not, when people lie, their statements offer the opportunity for rational scrutiny. The powerful might be better placed to cover their tracks, but it is rationality which suggests what they need to hide. Logical consistency and the logical determination of relevant evidence are enablements and constraints arising from language, not power. Truth claims have to be justified, not imposed (Thompson 1984: 70–1). This bears directly on the existence of the practices of science, rational law, medicine and the technologies. If we ask why they exist we do not get very far by deriving them from the dynamics of social power.

Rationality is an example of a constant of human existence which is 'mediated and given different emphases in different historical circumstances' (Crowther 1994: 161). Bourdieu regards all claims that there are such constants (universals) as ideologically motivated and to be explained by reference back to the social interests of the people making the claims. But though some claims to universality (classical political economy's 'laws of human nature', for example) may be so motivated and deserve to be relativized as ideology, there are others which do not. Rationality is a source of real differences – between truth and falsity no less – which cannot be equated with the difference between what does or does not give power to some social interest. This reinforces the claim that *real differences exist which are not simply effects of Bourdieu's 'difference producing principle', competition for social power.*

Aesthetic pleasure provides another example. Kant defined this as pleasure taken in the relations between the parts and the whole of a formal configuration. The possibility of paying attention to the formal qualities of objects for their own sake is a constant, arising out of the way objects impact on us. Humans are the kind of beings who can relate to objects in this way, appraising them for their beauty. When, where and by whom this may be done, and what they consider beautiful, is a matter of historical mediation. But real differences in objects and humans' capacity for their aesthetic evaluation are something for history to work on, not originate (Crowther 1994: 165). Aesthetic judgements about beauty can become the basis of social struggles and be used to mark 'distinction', but this does not mean that aesthetic differences themselves originate in social difference.

Historical production is, in part, grounded in 'constants in the self-consciousness of embodied subjects' more complex and more consequential for agency and structure than Bourdieu allows. But it is also grounded in the real differences generated within culture and practice. There are real differences between aesthetic and moral visions which do not correspond with differences of, and interests in, power. This is akin to the point about truth. Moral–cultural struggles are about securing normative approval for moral ideals. Ideal interests in, say, disciplining life according to a set of religious principles are no less real than material interests. Weber, from whom Bourdieu derives so much, recognized the irreducibility of religious interests and their constitutive force. Struggles over standards of cultural validity and the assertion and maintenance of cultural identities, centred on commitments to values and the meaning of certain symbols, cannot be reduced to interests in the distribution of an undifferentiated power. 'The peculiar tenacity with which the social groups hold onto their taste, cultures and forms of life in the face of historical changes and social transformations cannot be understood via . . . Bourdieu's utilitarian concept of action' (Honneth 1986: 64). Collectivization is not just a matter of being positioned in a distribution of power, but of being caught up in a world of values attracting commitment. Bourdieu regards the possibility of a 'committed subject' as illusory. But should we understand, say, the great world religions or the major contributions to philosophy, art and science as functioning only to secure social deference? 'Plainly not: Christianity as a cultural meaning-complex cannot be reduced to the mere authority of priests. Its world-historical role, across successive forms of social order, is not to be squeezed into any such straitjacket' (Anderson 1992: 153).

The upshot of this line of criticism is *not* to revert to subjectivism or idealism, but to encourage a more complicated sense of the objective grounds of subjectivity, agency and structure. Agents are socially produced all right, but are given access to sources of difference (biological, logical and cultural) which are necessarily in tension with the differences of social power. These sources stand as constants with the potential to challenge dominants' demands for deference. Whether or not such potential is realized is a matter of historical circumstances. By the same token, structures – relatively enduring patterns of social differentiation – are products of the commitments of agents far wider than to their interest in improving their standing in the distribution of power. To establish the interdependence of agency and structure successfully does not logically require us to embrace Bourdieu's agonistic and reductive metaphysics. Thinning out social subjects and objects to simplify their relations of mutuality into one of logical identity (both are the products of power) makes things easier, but comes with a stiff dose of disenchantment.

5

Giddens: Structuration through Knowledgeable Persons

Introduction: historical sociology

As noted in the opening chapter, Giddens introduced the term 'structuration' into contemporary social theory. This chapter considers the meaning he gives to it, and how it provides the basis for his elaboration of 'structuration' theory. First, I shall locate this theory within Giddens's overall sociological programme. Early interest in classical sociology produced two major texts, *Capitalism and Modern Social Theory* (1971) and *The Class Structure of the Advanced Societies* (1973). Subsequent work on the methodology of the social sciences, beginning with *Positivism and Sociology* (1974), saw the development of 'structuration' theory. The founding statement was *New Rules of Sociological Method* (1976) which was elaborated in *Central Problems In Social Theory* (1979). *A Contemporary Critique of Historical Materialism* (1981a) and the mature statement of *The Constitution of Society* (1984) followed. This period between 1974 and 1984 is often regarded as distinct, separated from Giddens's earlier interests and his later analysis of modernity in *The Consequences of Modernity* (1990a) *Modernity and Self Identity* (1991) and *Beyond Left and Right* (1994).

However, it is important to see all Giddens's output as disciplined by his belief that sociology must contribute to understanding the contemporary development of the modern world, and that classical sociology is not up to this task today (Giddens 1987: 166, 1990(b): 298, 1991; Tucker 1998: 1, 89). His strategy has been to modernize the nineteenth-century legacy of concepts and methods for producing sociology. His early work updates class theory, for example, while the period of 'structuration' theory is an investment in modernizing the methodological part of the legacy – the whole collection of ideas about the nature of social reality and how to investigate it. *A Contemporary Critique of Historical Materialism* (1981a) clearly demonstrates the function of the methodological phase for Giddens's lifelong project of using sociology to understand a developing modernity. Since then he has continued to defend his methodological ideas even though returning to the substantive analysis of contemporary modernity which motivated his earliest writings. Giddens is famous as a methodologist, but he has always seen himself, rightly, as an historical sociologist of modernity.

Analysing 'social systems'

Modernity is an example of a social system and for Giddens the disciplinary goal of sociology is to understand it. But this requires investigating what is involved in the historical–sociological analysis of social systems in general. By 'social systems', Giddens means any sets of practices, patterns of interaction and social relationships which are relatively enduring; 'system' in this context means no more than regularized, by being successfully reproduced, or integrated, over some period of time and space (Giddens 1981a: 42–3, 1984: 377, 1990b: 302). Historical sociology analyses the reproduction and transformation of such regularities (traditionally referred to as 'structures'). Historical sociology concerns itself with the development of all the traditional macroscopic objects of classical sociology, such as the development of capitalism, the state, rationality, bureaucracy, democracy etc. However, Giddens thinks it a mistake to associate the historical *only* with the macroscopic, or to see such large-scale phenomena as a distinct level of reality with its own processes. The micro–macro distinction is redundant, for even the most momentary social interaction is historically conditioned and contributes to the reproduction of the circumstances which gave rise to it (Giddens 1981a: 20). 'Structuration' theory investigates how 'the "supra-individual" *durée* of the long-term existence of institutions, the *longue durée* of institutional time' and 'the *durée* of daily life' intersect (Giddens 1981a: 19–20, 38, 44, 1981b: 173, 1984: 35).

Giddens seeks the sources of relatively enduring regularities of social systems and institutions in social interaction, which is at the same time both historically conditioned and historically productive. Centring on interaction subverts the nineteenth-century opposition between objectivism and subjectivism, neither of which is adequate on its own. To remind you; objectivism concentrates on the historical conditioning of interaction. It sees social systems as patterned, either by their external environments, or by their self-maintaining and self-transforming natures, whose operation can be expressed in terms of functional and evolutionary laws of development. People interact as effects of these laws. Social systems are systems in the strong sense, of having their own system-reproducing powers, whereas actors are agents only in the weak sense, of functioning as mediators of system-reproducing processes. Actors are constrained to become these functional agents by the system's socialization processes which mould their personalities and values to conform to the requirements of 'social order'. Actors are typically regarded as 'cultural dopes' who are normatively integrated. History is a natural process; social systems are produced by external and/or internal, natural forces. Giddens's main objectivist targets are Parsons's evolutionism and systems functionalism and the Marxist 'science of history' (Giddens 1977: 96–134, 1981a, 1984: 227–80). Though more sympathetic to Marxism, Giddens sees both as suffering from the scientific ambition to find some universal principle governing all historical development. This leads Parsons to formulate theory so vacuously as to be unfalsifiable and Marxism to make predictions which have not been fulfilled. Objectivist naturalism evidently has difficulty accommodating the variety and low predictability of social system developments. Giddens therefore rejects it, retaining only the interest in institutional development and the need to give some account of human agency.

Subjectivism, on the other hand, concentrates on the historical productivity of social interaction, crediting human beings with creative subjectivity, the capacity for voluntary, self-directing action. The non-natural realm of free will and meaning, of individuals and/or cultures, is seen as a powerful source of originality, generating the randomness of historical developments which so confounds objectivism. History is produced by the meaningful, intentional action of human subjects pursued in contexts of inter-action. Outcomes are the result of the combined effort of agents using their power to get what they want. This is the active principle of the subjectivist analysis of social system development. Typically, whatever social order exists is a temporary outcome of negotiation and is not given. Actors are socialized to be socially competent at participating in interaction, rather than normatively integrated. Actors are therefore agents in the strong sense, of bearing responsi-bility for outcomes, because, being free, they could have done other than they did, and systems are systems only in the weak sense, of exhibiting regularities. But this does not mean history is the *intended* consequence of their action. History is not directly willed by actors but is the unintended consequence of the multiplicity of their intended acts. This amounts to allowing that subjects' inten-tionality and the action informed by it are not that powerful. Though action is always present, to understand what happens requires particular historical analysis of the contingencies of the situation of action. Subjectivism has difficulty explaining the pat-terning and regularities social systems exhibit.

Giddens draws much from subjectivism, but he recognizes that an adequate social theory needs to (a) incorporate some elements of non-voluntary historical conditioning of action, (b) give some theoretical account of actors' subjectivity and powers of agency and (c) adequately account for social reproduction and the regularities of social systems (Giddens 1976: 22). We are now in a position to tackle his account of the structuration of social systems.

The fragility(uncertainty) of the social life of interacting persons

At the heart of Giddens's sociological imagination is a view of the nature and social predicament of human beings. This is the exis-tential foundation of 'structuration' theory and extends into his later work on modernity. Though not as explicit as it might be, it fuels his enthusiasm for hermeneutics, social phenomenology, Wittgenstein, ethnomethodology, Erikson, even Durkheim, but especially Goffman. These offer resources for accounting for how persons experience social interaction, particularly when faced with anxiety-producing *uncertainty* about *meaning*, the availability (*'presence' or 'absence'*) *of others*, and *interaction at a distance*. In the terms of his later work, it offers resources for understanding how people deal with risk.

For Giddens, social interaction occurs among individuals who, as selves, are 'objects to themselves' (Mead 1934: 136–7). 'The self is the agent characterised by the agent' (Giddens 1984: 43, 57). They have their own experience, but cannot make sense of it privately, needing to follow rules and submit to the judgement of some collectivity (Giddens 1976: 45). Sense depends on the interactional use of language to 'access' others' subjectivity. The subjectivity of selves is powerless without the media of intersubjectivity. Thus Giddens's thinking about social life places the person at the centre, as 'subject to be', sensing its dependence on others for the possibility of social interaction, through which it is constituted as a subject capable of meaningful action. In what might be called Giddens's 'methodological interactionism', persons ground their certainties in the direct, concrete experience of face-to-face interaction. Human being is defined by reference to participation in social interaction and not by the properties of individuals (Callinicos 1985: 143). Young children learn 'basic trust', which enables them to cope with the anxiety produced by the temporary absence of a parent – a paradigm of social experience. Only social interaction gives individuals access to language and an intersubjective context of use, which is the precondition of interpreting experience, and establishing meaning and knowledge. Only by being embroiled in a social world of others, with whom they can reliably interact, can persons have 'ontological security', that is a continuing sense of the well-foundedness of reality (Giddens 1984: 86–7, 375).

Thus, whatever is required to maintain the flow of interaction – what Giddens calls 'social integration' – is fundamental to the subjective agency of individuals. Goffman, Garfinkel and Schutz all show that knowledge and skills are required to 'make social life happen'; that these are essentially methodological procedures for maintaining the flow, the 'ongoingness', of interaction (Giddens 1981a: 19, 1996: 69). Fundamental to this accomplishment is 'monitoring one's behaviour in relation to that of others'. Giddens says 'there is no time out from this process which is simply chronic' (Giddens and Pierson 1998: 85). Face-to-face interaction is of prime importance because bodily 'co-presence' allows actors to register the unique details of context, gesture and demeanour (what Garfinkel calls 'indexicality') which help determine meaning (Giddens 1981a: 39, 1984: 82–3). The continuity of social life, and ultimately the persistence of social systems, is only secured by the continuous reflexive monitoring required by social interaction. This is the interactional condition of the hermeneutic circle, the condition of endlessly reviewing interpretations to determine their relevance in the light of changing circumstances.

Giddens adopts Heidegger's 'non-parametric conception of time/space' as consonant with his position (Giddens 1981a: 33; Gregory 1989: 192). Time/space relations are *constitutive* of all being, since being involves what Heidegger calls 'abiding in time' (Giddens 1981a: 31). Time and space do not exist 'in themselves but only as properties of extants', which, for Giddens, includes social systems (Giddens 1990b: 299). Time is four-dimensional: past, present, future and 'presencing'. In Giddens's formulation, 'Being exists in the coming-to-be of presence' (1981a: 31). For something to exist it has to be sustained, as a presence, manifesting its temporality. The times and locations of social interaction, employing skilful reflexive monitoring, are constitutive moments of the continuity, or 'presence', of social systems (Gregory 1989: 191).

Enabling historical agency; structures, 'knowledgeability' and 'capability'

The spatial and temporal regularization and extension of patterns of social interaction, the constitution of society, or system integration, is done by actors. But they are 'enabled' to exercise powers of historical agency, and 'transformative capacity', by having access to the prerequisites for human action which Giddens calls 'structures'. Language is paradigmatic of such structures which enable (or empower) actors to interpret, evaluate, influence and control elements of the situations in which they act. There are three 'modalities of structuration': signification, legitimation and domination. Thus actors use appropriate 'rules and resources' (structures) to give 'form' to situations of action by 'interlacing ... meaning, normative elements and power' (Giddens 1981a: 46–7, 1984: 28–9). Rules governing signification enable meaningful communication; those governing legitimation allow moral sanctioning. As for power, 'authoritative' and 'allocative' resources respectively allow command over people and over objects. Giddens uses 'structure' in the structuralist sense, of being generative. Structures, as 'rules and resources', do not do anything, but they have their effect through being known and used by actors. Mobilization to enable 'situated' or contextually specific activity establishes their existence. As potentialities they can have only a 'virtual' existence. They exist, in the sense of being present, in 'the generating moments of their constitution', or 'instantiation' (Giddens 1979: 5).

Subjective powers of agency therefore depend primarily on actors knowing how to do things, having a 'practical consciousness' of the appropriate rules for making sense of situations and a command of relevant resources. This 'practical consciousness' of 'knowing how to go on' depends on a wealth of taken-for-granted, 'mutual knowledge' about the routine requirements of the diverse contexts of activity. The vast bulk of human agency uses only this practical consciousness in contexts of routinized and familiar situations, where it is unnecessary to give reasons for what is being done. However, such reasons can generally be given, if required, using language directed by 'discursive consciousness'. This is involved whenever actors 'consciously confront a range of potential alternatives of conduct and make some sort of choice' among them (Giddens 1981b: 163). Giddens stresses the limited significance of such deliberate, premeditated choosing or 'intending', for agency. It is not that actors lack intentions and projects – seek no ends – but that their agency is an ongoing property of being caught up in interaction all the time. It is an agency of continual, practical 'presencing', or 'instantiation' of structures. Actors do not 'take time out' to decide *if* they will devote their agency to some end. Accounts of intention are generally produced during or after the activity they refer to, not before. 'Agency refers to doing' (Giddens 1981a: 16, 35, 1984: 9–10). Actors are agents because they could do otherwise but, being enmeshed in the routines of everyday life, they are generally repetitive, producing minor adjustments while following conventions (Giddens 1990b: 304). Historical agency is, to this very large degree, involuntary. It is a 'little' form of agency, one of knowing how to make use of historically given structures in situations which are the unintended consequences of earlier activity. Giddens rejects the grand or heroic form, the agency of free will and decision making, asserted by subjectivism.

The 'duality of structure'; constraint, enablement, and 'recursiveness'

We now come to what Giddens calls 'the crucial move' required to avoid objectivism and subjectivism (Giddens 1981a: 19). This is to conceptualize the relation between structure and agency as a 'duality', that is a relation in which neither of the related terms has any independent existence. Giddens talks of the 'duality of structure', though it is equally a duality of agency. Duality rules out subjectivism by conceptualizing agents' powers as dependent upon the use of structures comprised of rules and resources – the constraints which enable. Structures are the useable form of the past; 'Structures convey time. . .' (Giddens 1981a: 38). So agency is dependent on being knowledgeable about a legacy of ways and means of doing things. To the extent that it is made rule and resource-dependent, and past-dependent, it is objectified and conjoins subject and object.

But Giddens equally subjectivizes structures by seeing them as a 'virtual' reality whose existence is sustained, and whose generative force is realized, only through their practical, knowledgeable application by agents. Giddens defines structures as both 'the medium and outcome' of agency. They are outcomes because their use by agents has 'recursive' implications (Giddens 1981a: 27, 1984: 23–7). The recursiveness of agency is a *logical* entailment of 'drawing upon', using, or 'presencing', 'virtual' realities. Structures, as potentialities from the past, are kept in being by being used in the present. To act is necessarily to ensure that some rule or resource is repeated. Use is always 'using again'. Thus the continuity of structures involves agents' activation of the past in the present. Recursiveness, however, offers no logical guarantees about structures' future continuity. Only by being kept current can structures remain as potentialities to be drawn upon subsequently. It is important for understanding Giddens's general account of social reproduction and change that recursiveness should not be thought to 'load up the future'.

History without teleology

The 'duality of structure' implies that it is only the purposiveness of actors which activates structures and keeps them in being. History is not an end-seeking agent, which somehow pulls, or directs, present action so that it has particular consequences in the future. This teleological conception of history, typical of evolutionism, is rejected outright. For Giddens the future is 'open'. Several conditions guarantee this. **First**, what transpires will be the unpredictable outcome of the mix of intended and unintended consequences of the strategic use of structures by agents. In short it will be the result of the use of agents' power, and they could always do other than they did. Giddens insists that all agents, whatever their position in distributive hierarchies, have irreducible powers of agency; the principle of the 'dialectic of control' asserts that even the most severely subordinated interpret their situation and can influence how it impinges on them. Compliance with the existing order cannot be assumed (Giddens 1990b: 313). However, what happens will reflect the differential capabilities and competitive success, or power, of agents. **Second**, agents have to deal with situational contingency, that is the unique collection of circumstances within which they act, which is largely the unintended outcome of past agency. Agents are always applying structures in novel circumstances, modifying the structures perhaps, and producing outcomes which change the circumstances, intentionally and unintentionally. **Third**, the reflexivity of agents means they can change the knowledge which they use. Reflexive monitoring involves evaluation, critical appraisal and comparison of rules and resources; Giddens's agents can learn from mistakes and appropriate useful knowledge wherever they find it. Variation in the effectiveness of agents' 'knowledgeability/intentionality' is 'the erratic element' in human history (Giddens 1990b: 303).

Giddens believes: 'Change is intrinsic to every circumstance of social life' because of 'the inherent indeterminacy of social reproduction'. He says change is 'usually incremental . . . a slow drift away from a given practice or set of practices at any given location in time–space. Conventions become subtly modified in and through the ways in which they are "adhered to" – such change is by definition unintended and unplanned' (Giddens 1990b: 304). Here what is reproduced is the *changeful continuation* of social life as such, rather than the reproduction of any specific social form. However, Giddens recognizes that social practices are not, in fact, as random as his account of social agency in principle allows. Having condemned functionalism and evolutionism, how does he account for social occurrences, patterned activity, in terms of 'structuration'? (p. 308). Apart from the psychological need for routine, what are the processes making for the regularities that constitute social systems?

'Distanciation' is Giddens's term for the processes linking agency/structure with the development of social systems. When agents use structures they activate, or make present, social interaction and relations, which would otherwise be absent or virtual.

Rules and resources facilitate relating the immediate, momentary and proximate qualities of action situations, to what is more remote in time and space. Structures therefore 'stretch' situations and 'bind' them to others; 'distanciation' involves the 'dissolution of the restraints of time and space' (Giddens 1981a: 91). Using structures necessarily entails some element of *time–space extension*. Put differently, 'extension' means there will be regularities in the way interaction and social life are conducted, because the same structures are used at different times and places, thereby integrating, or binding, a multitude of encounters and the strategic activities of agents into the zoned regularities Giddens calls 'social systems'. Structures which become fundamental for organizing social interaction, such as 'tradition' and 'kinship', in the case of bands of hunter–gatherers, are 'structural principles', and can be used to typify societies (Giddens 1981a: 92–3, 1984: 376).

Giddens's agents necessarily engage in time–space extension and by implication have an *interest* in improving their capacity to 'extend' themselves beyond the present (Wright 1989: 98). This interest, implicit in Giddens's account, motivates the development of locales and techniques which increase 'storage capacity'; agriculture, food preservation, writing, education, cities, markets and states all enable agents to draw upon a wide and relatively reliable set of resources to cope with the contingencies of life. 'The expansion of storage capacity is the principal means of generating power in space–time distanciation' (Giddens 1981a: 100). All such 'remote' techniques work in tension with the 'goods' derived from proximate interaction. Agents, therefore, not only use structures, but use them to increase their power to make a difference at a distance, escaping the restrictions of intimate interaction.

Distanciation involves using resources to enhance resources. But this is not recursiveness, i.e. the logical reproduction of structures, entailed by their duality. It is a contingent matter of inventing appropriate storage techniques, motivated by an interest in the continuing supply of resources. This realistic emphasis on the problem of supply in human history recognizes that structures, insofar as they are resources, are not realized only in moments of instantiation, but can be contingently stored, rendered present but *un*used. The difference between a full barn and an empty one, as winter approaches, is concrete, not virtual. Giddens's discussion of storage, what Parsons calls 'latency', the maintenance of the capability of acting in the future, allows that agents try to 'load up the future' by enhancing their power to control outcomes. The problematic of storage implies that resources are not necessarily reproduced as they are used, and that the logical condition of recursiveness is not a guarantee of social reproduction. We need an analysis of the relation between the moments of use, and the moments of accumulation, of resources. Giddens's account of how structures are carried, in a virtual state, between contexts of use, is concentrated on the actors' memory and knowledge of rules, but this does not relate to material resources, which have their own temporalities. They are not carried in actors' minds and they are not virtual when not being used.

This tension in conceptualizing the reality of resources (and structure) and power in relation to instantiation and distanciation, points to the root difficulty for the internal coherence of Giddens's mode of 'structuration'. In relation to instantiation of structures, power is a logical property of all agents and is not determined by position in a social distribution of power or relations of domination (Giddens 1982: 197–9). Here, agency, defined as an ahistorical property of human beings, has indeterminate scope. It sounds as though a great deal is being claimed for agents, but equally it might be no 'big deal' at all (Callinicos 1985: 147). Giddens developed his 'duality of structure' understanding of the implications of resources for agency with reference to a particular kind of resource, language, which has no natural scarcity (Anderson 1983: 43–5; Callinicos 1985: 138). However, where resources are scarce, their relation to agency cannot be simply logical, but is one of the contingent access and distributional position of the actor. Relative scarcity of resources, the problem of supply and the pre-existence of resources, ignored in relation to instantiation are recognized by Giddens in the discussion of distanciation and domination. His very category 'allocative resources', giving command over objects, implies distributional variation. Here power is not simply an invariable, logical attribute of the category 'agents', but is socially distributed and struggled over, and is very much affected by the properties of the rules and resources which are used. In this light, agency must have variable scope, subject to access to 'stores' of resources and skill in their use. In any event, Giddens recognizes that resources (structures) are not simply internal to agency, as asserted by the 'duality of structure' principle, but pre-existing, objective, socially distributed conditions of action. Instantiation cannot be the only criterion of the existence of structures (Layder

1987: 26, 35). In particular, 'Distributions of power relations are logically and ontologically prior and external to instances of situated social activity' (Barbalet 1987: 4; Layder 1987: 38).

The central issue is the extent to which his account of distanciation finds Giddens acknowledging the durability, autonomous temporality and causality of social systems, which his 'structuration' programme was intended to deny. As Layder points out, 'the concept of system is often an ambiguous and sometimes contradictory element in structuration theory . . . it is meant to refer to reproduced social relations, that "stretch away across time and space", at the same time as it is called upon to conform to the instantiation criterion' (1987: 33–4). The duality of structure/agency, combined with time–space extension, simply recreates the dualism of subject and object, but this time between the duality of structure/agency on the one hand, and social system causality on the other. They are necessarily linked, because action requires resources (Barbalet 1987: 1). In other words, in Giddens's methodological writing, we are offered a dualism of instantiation and distanciation but with only *ad hoc* means for theorizing the relations between them, since the 'duality of structure' has been exhausted.

When Giddens tries to account for the structuration of historical development in his substantive historical sociology we find him constrained to supplement 'structuration' theory's concept of power in an *ad hoc* way. First, he shifts from theorizing power as a general transformative capacity of agents (who are never power*less*) to seeing it as a variable of social relations of domination and distributional hierarchies. Second, recognizing that power is *differentially distributed*, and is of *various kinds* (military, economic, ideological etc.), entails attributing relatively autonomous causality to properties of social systems. This opens the way for his historical sociology, implicitly at least, to suggest that social system development has some directionality. These features of Giddens's theorizing of historical structuration contradict the mere randomness implied by 'structuration' theory's methodological argument that social system change is no more than the contingent and unintended outcome of agency, that history has no developmental direction, and that, at every moment, anything is equally possible.

Does the distribution and specificity of kinds of power in institutional contexts of situated strategic action constrain it in a more determinate fashion than 'enablement'? Does power always, evenhandedly, enable and constrain as the duality relation demands?

Giddens's account of the logical and historical interaction of the three 'modalities of structuration' – signification, legitimation and domination – shows that he cannot remain consistent with his 'structurationist' principles and implicitly accepts that the kinds of power are not even-handed. He argues for the irreducibility of the agency of the socially weak, but shows it to be an agency which tends to reduce to the modalities of signification (codes) and legitimation (norms) – the consolation prize of the relatively powerless. The power of power relations lies in the modality of domination, the commanding of objects and people. That this modality has greater functionality is signalled by Giddens's classification of the resources of domination; 'allocative', involving the control of objects, and 'authoritative', involving the control of persons. His critique of Marxism's prioritizing of economic resources requires that he give them equal status, but is accompanied by his defining politics in terms of legitimation and confining allocation to objects, neglecting its nastiest mode, which could be described as the 'allocation' of people as objects. It is this power, the physical disposal of people by force, which emerges with a kind of 'ultimacy', as Giddens undertakes his historical sociology.

Indeed, correcting the neglect of violence by contemporary social theory becomes an important goal for Giddens's historical sociology (Giddens 1987: 167–8). Though not seeking to 'replace Marx with Nietzsche', he does embrace the Nietzschean and Weberian strain in social theory (Giddens 1981a: 3; Callinicos 1985: 134). Thus history really begins with the development of cities and their fusion into empires, early forms of state, which become the 'power containers' enabling ruling elites to store allocative, but more importantly, authoritative resources (Giddens 1981a: 92, 102–3, 1984: 181–5; Jary 1991: 125–7). Until the advent of capitalist class societies, military force, not economic necessity, is the predominant means of domination. The development of the state's ability to monopolize the use of force within its territory is the central narrative of Giddens's historical sociology (Jary 1991: 133). Capitalist development cannot take off until violence has been effectively excluded from economic activity. Early efforts to create 'homogeneous modes of administration and political allegiance within particular territories' are limited by communications and military technologies (Giddens 1981a: 102; Jary 1991: 126).

Without pursuing this account further, it is clear that it is committed to a systematic hierarchy of structures with violence at the top, as the most primitive. For early state builders there is no alternative to military action to integrate their social systems. They are externally constrained to wage war. Of course, their use of violence is mediated by their intentionality, skill and ambitions, but what they want and what they have to do to get it are highly predictable. Violence has a certain temporality, logic and ultimacy, since bodily integrity is at least as foundational for human agency as reflexive monitoring (Weber 1968: 54–5; Poggi 1990: 9–11). Moreover, the ever-present possibility of violence between humans means that it necessarily must be effectively controlled first, *before* the integration of 'class societies', using more abstract economic means such as money, commodified time and property law, can be successful (Giddens 1981a: 120; Jary 1991: 131). Though Giddens insists that history does not show continuous or unilinear development – the state development of 'class-divided society' is a necessary condition of the development of 'class society'. What this demonstrates is that Giddens finds himself assigning powers to structures to impose themselves on agents, and proposing nonrandom sequences of development. Though a long way short of teleology, Giddens does not manage to avoid directionality in social development and elements of systematicity stronger than his descriptive definition of 'social system' will tolerate (Wright 1989: 96–8).

PART THREE

Beyond the 'Structurationists'; Back to Reality

6

Archer:
'Structuration' and
the Defence of
'Analytical Dualism'

Introduction: refusing the 'structurationist' problematic

Archer has established a formidable reputation as a critic of Giddens's 'structuration' theory since the publication of her article 'Morphogenesis versus structuration: on combining structure and action' (1982). But she had already worked out the main lines of her alternative much earlier, in the introduction to her major work of historical sociology, *Social Origins of Educational Systems* (1979). The dates of its references suggest it was published some time after it was written; its 'Introduction' contains no reference later than 1973, and it clearly predates Giddens's *New Rules of Sociological Method* (1976). Archer does use the term structuration in that discussion, but very definitely in the first sense described in Chapter 1. Her purpose in *Social Origins* was to defend the macro-sociological analysis of social systems against methodological individualism. She then transferred much of her critique of the latter to her attack on 'structuration' theory (which I have described as 'methodological interactionism'). Archer sees 'structuration' theory as guilty of the same weaknesses as methodological individualism, and as constituting a similar threat to the kind of social analysis which she thinks is scientifically and politically irreplaceable.

Archer pursues her original position with clarity and consistency. She elaborates and deploys it against Bourdieu and Giddens, establishes an alliance with Bhaskar's realist philosophy of social science, but does not change it in any major way. While undoubtedly motivated to propound her position continually in response to these initiatives, it had its own independent origin in the 1950s Anglo-American analytical philosophical debates about social theory. These centred on *explanatory methodology*; how best to conceptualize the individual/society relation in order to explain social phenomena and individual action. Archer often talks of 'grappling' with reality, and the test of explanatory usefulness dominates her social theory. Her social theoretical perspective is that of a practising social analyst who has no doubts that what sociologists and historians actually do is well founded. The only problem is to make that foundation explicit.

The 1950s debate was structured by a dichotomy between two exclusive options: explanation in terms of 'individuals' or in terms of 'social wholes' (corresponding to the subjectivism/objectivism divide discussed in Chapter 1). 'Methodological individualists' (most notably Watkins 1957) developed their arguments against 'methodological holists', who were convicted of reifying social entities. Methodological individualists' ontological position, based on an empiricist epistemology, denied that social system concepts referred to something real. What existed was what could be directly observed and, since only individuals could be observed in this way, they alone were real. Critics, notably Gellner (1956), while seeking to avoid reification, defended the existence of social realities which could not be reduced to, or derived from, individuals. They showed the impossibility of describing individuals without presuming the existence of some non-individual social reference. Associating herself with this social realism, Archer sought to strengthen the ontological defence of the existence of social systems (Archer 1996: 680). At the heart of her project is the commitment to avoid reifying social systems while defending their reality. This requires conceptualizing individuals and social systems as both distinct and different from, but also as interdependently related to, each other. She therefore refuses the exclusive options of the 1950s debate in order, as we will see, to develop a humane, non-mechanical account of social systems, which will help people understand where best to direct their efforts to take control of their lives. Her willingness to espouse some form of social systems theory in the early 1970s suggests a significant degree of independence from the influence of the 'structurationist' moment. Archer acts as a major carrier of the social theory of the 1950s into the 1980s, relatively unaffected by the experience of fragmentation to which Giddens responded. She is a leader of a 'neo-traditionalist revival' (McLennan 1995: 117). For Archer, if the lessons of the most sophisticated debates of the 1950s had been properly learned, coherence and integration might have been maintained and Giddens's work of synthesis would have been unnecessary.

Conceptualizing social systems: living with the past

Archer's position depends on a concept of social system which she claims is not reified; that is, not thought of as a 'thing' with self-moving powers in the manner of classical evolutionism or systems functionalism. The choice is not between 'action' and 'system', but between a strong concept of social system which is nevertheless dependent on action and one that asserts systems' entire independence from action. Archer has always regarded the polarization of action and system, famously described by Dawe (and embraced by Giddens in opposing objectivism to subjectivism) as 'Manichean' and unnecessary – the result of failing to think subtly enough about the reality of social systems (Archer 1979: 21). Archer thinks the term system can be used in ways which are not mechanistic, deterministic or dehumanized, offering a conceptualization which, while relating it to action, neither reduces the latter nor is reduced by it. She only insists that systems (a) are relatively autonomous, (b) pre-exist agents, and (c) are causally efficacious, and that these claims do not entail reification.

Chapter 1 showed that, for dualists, the relation between structure and agency is one of *non-identity*. This stance ensures that *the relation itself* is analytically distinguishable from what is related by it. Relations do real work connecting the logically distinct identities of structure and agency, and what that work is has to be established. By contrast, where structure and agency are seen as a 'duality' there *is* no analytically separate relation between them to be investigated. Dualism is the typifying mark of Archer's thinking and distinguishes her from Giddens: she seeks to develop concepts of the *various* relations between structure and agency which help explain why particular cases are the way they are.

All explanatory methodologies used to do practical social analysis are regulated by some social ontology i.e. theory of the generic properties of social realities (Archer 1995: 5, 1998a: 72). Ontological distinctions define the kinds of elements explanations can mobilize. Such elements will have a capacity to exert some degree of independent influence on the social process of structuration. Ontological social theory therefore defines the elements which have 'relative autonomy', but leaves open if, and how exactly, they are related in each case. Practical analysis involves investigating this. For Archer, social theory orchestrates the investigation of relations in reality and should not foreclose consideration of any possible avenues of relatedness. She objects to methodological individualism and 'structuration' theory because they remove the analytically useful difference between 'agency' and 'system', making it impossible to address the variable form of the relation between them. Her programme for macro-sociology is the study of the production and transformation of such variable forms, that is *morphogenesis*.

Fundamental to this approach is the distinction between Archer's methodological 'analytical dualism' described above, and 'philosophical dualism', arguing for an ontological separation of individual and society, which she rejects (Archer 1996: 680). Her analytical dualism accepts that there are no social realities without people, that these realities manifest themselves in the behaviour of people, and that we must be 'descriptive individualists'. 'No people, no society', as she puts it, summarizes her *anti-dualist ontology*. But it is precisely because individuals and society, structure and agency are inseparable coexistants that it is necessary to have a *dualistic explanatory methodology* which distinguishes them analytically, allowing their variable relations to be investigated. Morphogenesis is therefore about change in *the form of the relation and its consequences, not whether or not a relation exists*. Ontologically, structure and agency are necessarily related; analytically they must be distinguished to establish what the relation is.

As the title of her early work suggests, a morphogenetic approach thinks of systems, such as education systems, as historical outcomes of social processes. Archer follows Blau, Buckley, Gouldner and especially Lockwood, all of whom analyse the relations between interaction, its outcomes and its conditions, which are themselves the outcomes of earlier interaction. Lockwood's distinction between social and system relations involves seeing reality as *stratified into kinds*, each with their own *internal* relations. Systems are *emergent* outcomes of periods of social interaction between actors, who use their power to try to get their preferences. Systems are those outcomes of agency which 'emerge' or pass a developmental threshold, beyond which they exercise their own causal powers, independently of the agency which produced them. This autonomy, once brought into existence by actions, *conditions* future action in specific ways (which the sociologist must identify) but this conditioning is *not* determination. If it were, full-blooded agency would be surrendered.

These notions of a 'stratified reality', 'emergence' and 'conditioning' are of fundamental importance to Archer's project. 'Emergence' allows for activity-dependence of structures/systems, but also their acquisition of autonomous properties. 'Conditioning' allows these acquired autonomous properties of structures subsequently to constrain action, but without so overwhelming the agency of actors that they cannot affect outcomes. The powers of actors and systems are both strongly asserted and equally strongly limited by being related in temporal sequence. Above all, though systems are more than simply descriptive regularities and have systematic constraining or conditioning properties, they do not have self-producing powers analogous to those of a biological system. Archer firmly distinguishes her concept of system from that of 'equilibrium theory' (systems or normative functionalism) in which systems are thought of teleologically, as having preferred states towards which they tend (Archer 1979: 25–42, 1982: 457).

Morphogenetic analysis proceeds by framing a field of investigation in terms of an analytical temporal sequence. First, there is *conditioning* by all pre-existing conditions, the given state of affairs, of the social action being investigated. Then there is a present of *social interaction* in which agents try to achieve their goals using their powers. And finally there are the outcomes of this episode of interaction, which may result in *structural elaboration* of the conditions of action, including the agents themselves. These changed structures and agents then become the conditions for future action – and so on endlessly. The concerns of micro- and macro-sociologists are combined, for the outcomes of interaction and agency have emergent relational properties that are different from those of the individuals and interaction that produced them. These properties are relatively durable relations (historical, systemic or 'macro') which condition subsequent interaction, but are open to become the target of (individual, agentic or 'micro') efforts to reinforce or transform them. Thus actors cannot avoid being constrained by structures but they can do something about the specific form the constraints take. They are the agents of historical change. If we join Archer in wanting to explain why England, France, Russia and Denmark have different state education systems, the answer must take the form of comparative analytical history. This shows how the different historical legacies of each conditioned the educational ideas and political action of those engaged in the struggles to set up such systems, resulting in different sorts of structural elaboration of what was already there (Archer 1979: 44). The relation of agency and structure is intrinsically temporal and historical: it is this condition which allows Archer to say that the powers of each must always be considered, but that their precise force has to be established case by case.

Archer claims that Weber provided the prototype for this approach, by recognizing that, though action is always undertaken in a preformed structural context, such contexts are not necessarily tightly integrated and typically offer opportunities for actors to innovate and change the direction of development (pp. 5–8). This is consistent with recent assessments which show how Weber avoids the dualism of micro/macro and relates the relatively autonomous elements of agency and structure (Kalberg 1994). Archer's position maximizes openness to possibilities; a minimum of analytical distinctions is made, allowing the greatest possible variation in concrete cases. Neither oppressive structural constraint, where conditioning seems like determination and actors are caught in the embrace of fully integrated systems, nor the self-determination of well-resourced, talented, politically emancipated individuals working the structures to their advantage, are ruled out. Contingency, the contradictoriness and hence openness of structures, and the skills, imagination and effort of individuals (and hence the openness of agency) all have a bearing on emergent outcomes and whether or not structures are reproduced or transformed in some way. The goal of analysis is to discover how relevant factors are related, not to decide the issue, theoretically, in advance. But the most important characteristic of this approach is that systems can only be conceptualized as real, without reification, by relating them to the agentic powers of individuals over time. Analytically speaking, the relation between agency and structure is one of historical alternation between the conditioning of agents by structure and the elaboration of structure by interacting agents. Given time, systems can be both cause and caused, as can agency. Analytical dualism depends on temporality (Archer 1996: 694).

The critique of the 'structurationists': process without system and 'sociology in the present tense'

I have suggested Archer developed her basic position to defend the value and practicality of macro-sociology against methodological individualism. She argues one can talk about social system properties, without reification, by showing them to be emergent, relatively autonomous products of the action of individuals. Social systems, though produced by actors, acquire powers that are not those of the individuals who produced them, nor of those whom they condition. Her main argument against individualism is that, if there are no social forces independent of individuals, there is no way the products of the past activity of individuals can exercise any constraint in the present. If individuals are the only medium of constraint, then it becomes impossible to influence the future after the action (and even life) of the agent is over. The present can have no influential past and, by the same token, cannot affect the future. Archer argues that social system concepts are necessary to conceptualize the mechanisms, or 'carriers', of the past's influence, since individuals alone are insufficient to account for it. Individualism is forced to imagine life lived disconnected from the past, constrained only by whatever individuals in the present choose to work with. As Archer puts it, there is 'a curious suspension of the time scale' and loss of historical depth (Archer 1979: 11–12). Social systems necessarily entail this depth. If we accept that the past constrains us independently of the agency of specific individuals in the present, then macro-sociological concepts are necessary. Methodological individualism only avoids such concepts by compressing time into the present, thereby weakening explanatory capacity. A similar compression is the target of her attack on Giddens's 'structuration' theory as formulated in *Central Problems in Social Theory* (Giddens 1979).

But though Giddens is her major target, Archer's criticism of Bourdieu's account of educational practice is also instructive. He argues that a universal 'logic of pedagogic action' explains what goes on in classrooms and why its effects are generally reproductive of the social system. Archer objects for three reasons. First,

Bourdieu reduces the structuration of education to one level, that of pedagogic interaction, ignoring the influence of wider educational politics and institutions. He treats differences between national education systems as irrelevant for explaining the reproduction or transformation of educational practice, thereby denying the relative autonomy of systems. He generalizes the French system, ignoring the different conditions of action between centralized (France) and decentralized systems. Second, he neglects the history of educational politics and struggle which produced the systems in the first place. Without this history of human agency, Bourdieu is left with a blatant systems functionalism; educational practice is the way it is because it is functional for the survival of the system. Third, his analysis denies the agents of educational practice – teachers, students, parents etc. – any capacity (relative autonomy) to resist or steer the direction of development. The whole analysis is mechanical rather than historical. The system is fully integrated and there is no distinction between system and social integration. Above all, the analysis is *vague* about *who* is responsible for important decisions, and *when* elements of the systems are established. The autonomy of systems and agents is eliminated by the absence of temporality – the time of events, institutionalization and emergence (Archer 1983, 1993). Bourdieu's analysis, for Archer, is typical of the 'structurationist' compression of levels of reality at which autonomous powers emerge, and the shrinking of temporality into present interaction.

This compression is central to her relentless pursuit of Giddens's 'structuration' theory, which, beginning in the 1982 article, 'Morphogenesis versus structuration . . .' (revised in 1985 and 1990), became the basis for all her subsequent contributions to social theory. Archer and Giddens agree that the war between objectivism and subjectivism must be ended because: 'action and structure presuppose one another: structural patterning is inextricably grounded in practical interaction'. They both see social practice as ineluctably shaped by the unacknowledged conditions of action and as generating unintended consequences which form the context of subsequent interaction. Both hold that the 'escape of human history from human intentions, and the return of the consequences of that escape as causal influences upon human action, is a chronic feature of social life' (Giddens 1979: 7; Archer 1990: 74). But agreement that the goal of social theory was to relate structure and agency leads straight to the profoundest disagreement about how that relation should be conceptualized to avoid objectivism and subjectivism. Archer thinks 'structuration' theory's way of doing so, by asserting the identity of structure and agency, is the wrong way because it is utterly useless for understanding structuration.

We have seen Archer asserting structure and agency's *differences of kind* and relative autonomy in a stratified social reality, and the potential variety of their forms of relation. She calls herself an 'emergentist', opposing herself to Giddens's 'conflation' or 'elision' of the elements to be related. For Archer, 'conflation is always an error in social theory'. Just as objectivism and subjectivism conflate structure and agency by reification or reduction, Giddens conflates them by 'depriving both elements of their relative autonomy, not through reducing one to the other, but by compacting the two together inseparably' (Archer 1996: 688). They are 'clamped together in a conceptual vice' (Archer 1990: 78). Giddens responds to the Manichean polarization of structure and agency with an equally extreme insistence on their identity. This is because, though wanting to retain structure, he is intimidated by the danger of reification. The elision (conflation) of 'structuration' theory involves

> a *decentering of the subject* . . . Because human beings become people, as opposed to organisms, only through drawing upon structural properties to generate social practices, [and] there is an equivalent *demotion of structure*, which becomes real, as opposed to virtual, only when instantiated by agency . . . neither structure nor agency have independent or autonomous features, but only properties which are manifested in, and reproduced or transformed through, 'social practices'.
>
> (Archer 1996: 687, my emphasis)

The difference between the emergentist/analytical dualist/morphogenetic position and that of the elisionist/duality/'structurationist' is obvious. Archer's social theory involves *promoting structure* and *recentring agency*.

As we have seen, the key to this is the way time is incorporated into the relation. The difference between the two approaches is, at root, between two attempts to imagine the *temporal form* of the interrelation between structure and agency in social life. Archer describes 'structuration' theory as follows;

> [It] involves an image of society, not as a series of acts, but as a continuous flow of conduct which changes or maintains a potentially

malleable social world. In turn it obviously proscribes any discontinuous conceptualisation of structure and action – the intimacy of their mutual constitution defies it . . . Because of the dynamic interplay of the two constituent elements, structuration does not denote fixity, durability, or even a point reached in development. Structuration itself is ever a process and never a product.

(Archer 1982: 457, 1990: 75)

Process, flow, continuity, and the ever-present possibility of 'making a difference' preoccupy Giddens's utopian imagination. For him social theory must incorporate time, in order to conceptualize the moment-by-moment constitution of society by the duality of structure/agency.

The morphogenetic imagination, by contrast, seeks to establish the various ways the past constrains action in the present, and how that same action can effect those constraints. Time is necessary to conceptualize the historical depth of social existence. This difference, between an intimate, mutual constitution of structure and agency in the present, and an historically deep, sequential interplay of relatively durable fixities and human agency, of products and processes, is fundamental. For Archer, historical development is not necessarily a smooth flow: the French education system, for example, has a 'stop–go history of change' (Archer 1993: 236).

The 'duality of structure' dissolves the difference between structure and agency and 'overcomes' the associated dichotomies (fundamental to the morphogenetic approach) 'between voluntarism and determinism, between synchrony and diachrony, and between individual and society' (Archer 1982: 458). Archer's point is that losing such distinctions makes practical social analysis impossible. Doing social theory by amalgamating elements from contemporary schools of thought achieves only a rhetorical integration and is unhelpful for practical analysis. Giddens's logical redefinition of structure and agency removes the possibility of analysing their historical relation – as shown by his term for the process of realizing structures, 'instantiation'. Moreover, by defining structure as 'rules and resources', agents are enhanced by being constrained only by what enables them to act. The plasticity of structures to agency is built into the definition. Giddens's actors are 'hyperactive' and 'enjoy very high degrees of freedom' (Archer 1990: 77). At the same time, by claiming that any use of structures recursively reproduces them, he is 'committed to an enormous coherence of the structural properties'. Actors cannot escape

contributing to reproduction as every bit of their behaviour is implicated in it. Archer shows how the 'duality of structure' only com-
bines the originally contradictory elements. But her chief objection
is that Giddens cannot even pose, let alone answer, questions about
when actors can change things and when they cannot, about variations in the strength of constraints, or what gives people more or
less freedom (pp. 78–9). Central to the morphogenetic approach is
the temporal distinction of constraint and freedom. Structural
constraints may have specific durations, simply by virtue of what
they are, as objective and concrete realities. They do not depend
for their constraining effect on being instantiated and are not actor-
dependent once they have fully emerged. The doctrine of 'instantiation' flatly contradicts the doctrine of emergent relative
autonomy.

Promoting structure and recentring agency. Developing Lockwood's legacy: parts and people

Fundamental to analytical dualism and the critique of elision/con-
flation is Lockwood's insistence that social reality comprises two
kinds of relations, the systemic and the social – Archer's relations
between 'parts' and 'people'. But she realizes that the case for
realism also requires specifying what is irreducible about each,
what gives them their powers to affect outcomes, in combination
with each other. Central to her account is that *both* the sys-
temic/structural and agentic/human elements of the historical
process are subject to the emergence of new forms, relations and
powers. Emergence is not just characteristic of structures. Morphogenesis is double. The exercise of agency potentially changes *all*
the conditions of agency, including agents themselves (Archer 1995:
173–7).

Archer develops Lockwood by identifying three kinds of emergent, the structural, cultural and agential, each having its own irreducible kind of *internal relations* with their own 'natural necessity'
(Sayer 1992: 169–71). The structural and cultural correspond to the
'parts' and the agential to the 'people'. The natural necessity of the
internal relations gives each kind of emergent its relative autonomy to contribute to the process of structuration (reproducing or
transforming conditions). All three have the properties of pre-
existence, autonomy, durability and causal efficacy (see Figure 6.1).

Thus Archer's 'structural' refers to the internal relations of the

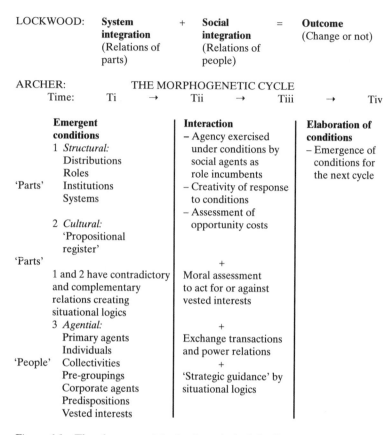

LOCKWOOD: **System**   +   **Social**   =   **Outcome**
             integration   **integration**   (Change or not)
             (Relations of   (Relations of
             parts)   people)

ARCHER: THE MORPHOGENETIC CYCLE
        Time: Ti   →   Tii   →   Tiii   →   Tiv

Emergent conditions	**Interaction**	**Elaboration of conditions**
1 *Structural:* Distributions Roles	– Agency exercised under conditions by social agents as role incumbents	– Emergence of conditions for the next cycle
'Parts' Institutions Systems	– Creativity of response to conditions – Assessment of	
2 *Cultural:* 'Propositional register'	opportunity costs	
'Parts'	+	
1 and 2 have contradictory and complementary relations creating situational logics	Moral assessment to act for or against vested interests	
3 *Agential:* Primary agents Individuals	+ Exchange transactions and power relations	
'People' Collectivities Pre-groupings Corporate agents Predispositions Vested interests	+ 'Strategic guidance' by situational logics	

Figure 6.1   The elements of Archer's analytical dualism

material dimension of social life, involving the distribution of resources, the mutual implications of roles, institutional positions and their internal coordination and, at the most general level, relations among institutions. This is the emergence of hierarchies and divisions of labour. These are kinds of material conditions with their own 'natures', distinct from the properties of the people who occupy the positions and roles, that exercise an independent influence on outcomes. Archer argues it is quite inadequate to collapse this kind of relatively autonomous contributor to the structuration process into instantiation on the basis of knowledgeability, as 'structuration' theory does (Archer 1995: 177). Structures constrain, whether anybody actually recognizes this or not. As we shall see, they constrain and enable the projects of agents by creating differential opportunity costs for people in different positions, and consequently vested interests in change or stability for those sharing a position of relative advantage or disadvantage (Archer 1990: 87–8, 1995: 196–211).

The other kind of 'part' is the cultural. This refers only to the relational properties of cultural products which exercise objective constraint independently of what people actually believe. As with structure, this kind of 'part', produced by agents' interaction, can acquire independence from them by virtue of its internal relations. Culture, whatever can be understood by someone, acquires autonomy from people when cast into propositional form, becoming subject to the universality of the law of non-contradiction (Archer 1995: 180). Then it can be evaluated independently of given agents. Establishing a proposition's truth is not a process of sociocultural interaction to persuade people to believe it. Most of what we normally call culture is insufficiently separated out from interaction into propositional form to exercise its own relatively autonomous power over agency. It is nonetheless true that, as with structure, agency is conditioned by a 'propositional register' of theories, beliefs and values which pre-exist moments of interaction.

Every structural and cultural 'part' of social reality, say an institution or a theory, has its internal relations (first order emergents). There are also relations within and between both kinds of 'parts' (second order emergents) as when institutions are related to each other and to cultural elements. Second order emergents may be contradictory or complementary, and necessary or contingent. They imply 'situational logics'. For example, the necessary contradiction of a state which both defends and taxes private property being simultaneously a friend and enemy of private ownership cannot be removed. It has to be lived with and a compromise struck. Contingent contradictions, on the other hand, may be rectified; for instance, blind people's inability to see light signals, which undercuts the intention that their installation help all pedestrians, can be remedied by adding sound signals. In the case of complementary relations, where things fit well together, the necessary can be cherished and protected, and the contingent exploited as a bit of good fortune. Thus in general terms structure constrains agency by setting opportunity costs for agents and by presenting them with situational logics, which provide them with 'strategic guidance' (Figure 6.2).

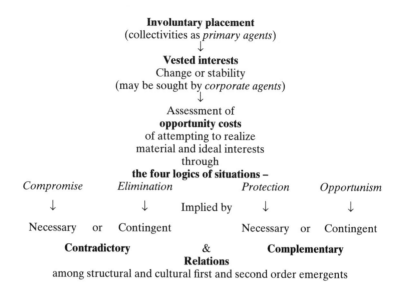

Figure 6.2   Structural sources of agency; vested interests and the logics of situations

Finally there are the emergent, conditioned and conditioning, properties of people. Archer specifies all the different kinds of relations in which they are formed and through which they contribute to structuration, distinguishing analytically between persons, social agents and actors. She starts what she calls her 'stratified' model of people by insisting that human beings are a 'natural kind' with distinct presocial biological features (Archer 1995: 287–9). As babies they relate to an undifferentiated object-world on the basis of biological relations; needs for food, warmth etc. and with a capacity to learn, and to develop a continuous sense of self (pp. 282–93). The 'sense of self' of *persons* is 'the indispensable human element which contributes to social life'. This is presocial, enduring, autonomous and causally efficacious, and must not be absorbed by the concept of self, which is social and highly changeable. So far then, we have 'the body plus the continuity of consciousness' as the determinate human material with presocial proclivities (Archer 1995: 126). Concepts of social identity refer to people already possessing continuous, embodied, personal identities. The self and its emergent personality is what the social impinges upon to constitute persons as social agents.

It does so initially by 'involuntarily placing' the person in the relations among collectivities emergent from distributions of scarce resources and positions. People are unavoidably constituted as *'primary agents'* of the vested interests of some collectivity since they must relate to the world through material stratification systems (Archer 1995: 253–7). To become what Archer terms a *'corporate agent'* involves actively participating in, and elaborating, the relations between collectivities, using organizational resources (means) and with reasons for acting in one way rather than another (interests or 'ends') (p. 130). Ends are 'derandomized' (Parsons) because being a social agent necessarily entails having a point of view from which to assess opportunity costs and strategic logics. However, that assessment also depends on the autonomous properties of persons, who can opt to act for, or against, their collectivity's vested interests. Interests are subject to social necessity, but there is no compulsion to adopt them. The interests and desires that actually motivate action are thus only partly decided by the 'external reasons' supplied by the vested interests of collectivities in the social structure. Structure sets an agenda, but this is positively related to on the basis of the 'internal reasons' supplied by the self-reflection of each person (Archer 1995: 129–31). All that Archer claims for the autonomy of persons and social structures is that, though persons can decide to act against the tendencies of their social position, choosing to promote the interests of others (i.e. altruism) will always have a price, set by that position (Archer 1990: 88).

The second way the social impinges on people is through the array of roles which they can occupy, thereby becoming *social actors*. Roles offer possibilities for individuals, as unique persons, to 'make a difference'. Unlike positions in distributions, roles can be chosen, but only on the basis of assessing the opportunity costs involved. There is freedom to choose within the patterning process because, as autonomous persons, people can take on high costs and risks for their ambitions (Archer 1995: 276–8). As a role-incumbent a person 'personifies' the role, exploiting its plasticity, elaborating it, motivated by interests and desires which are partly social and partly personal in origin. The *way* roles are performed and expectations satisfied is framed by social agency but not determined by it. Similarly there is freedom to identify with a role, making it central to the actor's social self, or not. People have to occupy roles but these may be at odds with their personal identities.

This picture of people as *agents* of stratified collectivities, on the basis of which they become *actors* in roles, both elements being 'anchored' in the humanity of *persons*, allows relative autonomy to all three. The social 'parts' impinge on the 'people' who, as persons with non-social properties (their biology, their direct private experience, and their continuous 'sense of self') have the power to decide how they respond to their social options. That is why social reality is an 'open system'. But though prediction is ruled out, conditioning tendential effects of differential opportunity costs and situational logics provide a basis for explaining the patterning of action and preferences. Simultaneously, the full-blooded acceptance of the autonomy of personhood allows for the explanation of those who act against type (Archer 1995: 252).

Conclusion

This brief outline is sufficient to show what a fully relational, emergentist and dualist social theory involves. Archer puts the elements of social theory through a process of 'decompression' to isolate the relatively autonomous elements of social reality. 'Autonomy' means that they can exercise an independent influence on the process of structuration, but 'relativity' means that this influence operates through relations of dependence upon the other relatively autonomous elements. So, given time, each is conditioned and conditions. Subjects are recentred and structures reinstated; but it is precisely because very strong claims are made for each that sole responsibility for outcomes cannot be attributed to either. This is Archer's tactic for escaping objectivism and subjectivism, and offering guidance for practical social analysis, whose business is to show how relations between subjective and objective elements of social realities are encountered in historically specific concrete cases. Archer's concept of agency 'bridges the gap between personal reality and a social reality which conditions objective life-chances and therefore the adopting of roles. Thus something general but determinate (opportunity costs, vested interests and situational logics) is offered to practical analysis about how structure impinges on actors' (Archer 1995: 292–3). This provides the tools for achieving precision about agency by encouraging us to look for *who* did what, and *when*.

It is this historical precision which is so conspicuously absent from 'structuration' theory, which conceptualizes agency as equi-possible for everyone, at every moment, on the grounds that everyone engages in practice and uses rules and resources on the basis of knowledgeability. As an existential 'given' of individuals nobody can fail to be an agent (Thompson 1989: 74; Archer 1995: 117–18). We might be willing to accept this as an ontological proposition about human existence, but such a generous concept of agency is not useful for the analysis of structuration. Fundamental to dualist social theory then, is a less socially vacuous concept of agency, one which differentiates between people in terms of their power and responsibility for what actually happens. And that means concep-tualizing agency as dependent on structurally conditioning factors which differentially distribute the capacity to influence outcomes.

7

Mouzelis: The Restructuring of 'Structuration' Theory

Introduction

Mouzelis has developed his own critique and alternative to 'structuration' theory which runs parallel to Archer's project and shares much with it, though, as we shall see, there are differences of emphasis and argumentation. Mouzelis is more conciliatory towards the ideas he criticizes, and develops his own theory by synthesizing positive elements he finds in them. But, with Archer, his intention is to defend the possibility of historical or 'macro'-sociology (Mouzelis 1991: 4). Sociological theory is to provide the conceptual tools for sociology to fulfil its task of showing 'how social wholes are constituted, reproduced and transformed' (Mouzelis 1995: 150). Since this task requires conceptualizing social systems as relatively enduring realities, which can be distinguished from the human beings who produce them and are conditioned by them, Mouzelis is committed to asserting the objective dimension of social reality and hence social theoretical dualism. This is his fundamental position despite his partial support for Giddens's notion of the 'duality of structure'.

Like Archer, Mouzelis approaches the 'crisis' of contemporary sociological theory on the basis of earlier substantive work – in his case on the theory of organizations and the comparative historical sociology of 'semi-peripheral' countries, among which is his native Greece. *Organisation and Bureaucracy* (1967, 1975; the dates here are significant) analyses theories of the objective properties of organizations, administrative techniques, decision-making environments and hierarchies. Organizations are vertical and horizontal arrangements of positions and offices which are systematically related to one another. How they are related has consequences, and social systems analysis can address the functionality of organizational design. Organization confers on collectivities the capacity to act; it coordinates a number of people by specializing role structures and concentrating decision making in particular positions. The 'parts' of such systems are operated by incumbents who relate to their positions, and to each other, not only on the basis of their intraorganizational experiences but also in terms of what they bring from outside the organization, and their personal qualities. Since actors are not passive there must be organizational politics, conflicts of interest, differences arising from the way the rules are interpreted, and so on. Organization theory raises the issue of differences between the way systems are designed and actually operate when, as Archer would put it, 'peopled'. It also points to differences of power and importance which individuals acquire from their position in hierarchies. Mouzelis draws on all these themes in his later critique of sociological theory.

Resisting reductionism

Mouzelis's early substantive work resists three major forms of reductionism in sociology: the reduction of system/collective realities to individual actors, the reduction of historical processes and contexts to internal systems relations, and the reduction of the political and cultural to the economic, typical of Marxism. We will take each in turn.

In the light of the theoretical turmoil of the late 1960s as the 'orthodox consensus' was variously challenged (see Chapter 1), Mouzelis prefaced the second edition of *Organisation and Bureaucracy* with a new, self-critical introduction. However, there is one uninterrupted commitment which is clear from his *defence of the idea of collective actors against the charge of reification*. Provided one can, in principle, spell out the social processes of coordination, decision making and representation, it is perfectly proper to speak of the goals, intentions and strategies of non-individuals.

Reification occurs only when system-related concepts are credited with the properties that individuals or groups alone can have, 'when one treats parts as actors' (1975: xvi) as Parsons does. Mouzelis insists on this *strict criterion of reification* in order to allow system and collective action concepts, and avoid the individualistic voluntarism so popular in the early 1970s. Though opposing reification, his predominant interest is *resisting the reduction* of the collective concepts used by historical sociologists to analyse large-scale and long-term processes. This was exactly Giddens's intention when first developing his critique of interpretative sociologies and insisting on retaining some concept of structure, albeit only in the virtual form of 'structuration' theory (1976).

Mouzelis continues to talk about social systems and collective actors in a non-reductive way. But his new introduction now also challenges organization theory's focus on how organizations work and its tendency to emphasize relations among system parts, at the expense of relations with the 'exterior', spatial and historical context and the origins of organizations (1975: 178). Rejecting such ahistorical analysis, Mouzelis now criticizes his earlier failure to situate Weber's ideal type of bureaucracy within the latter's wider comparative analysis of historical forms of administration. This is the first of many references to the exemplary status of contemporary historical sociology represented by Moore, Lipset, Anderson, Wallerstein, Braudel, Mann, Skocpol and others (the list varies) all of whom, like Archer, follow in Weber's footsteps (1975, xxiii, 1978: 70, 1991: 58, 67–70, 123, 160, 1995: 42–3). Weber developed his 'model' of bureaucracy, as a conceptual tool for analysing the development of the characteristic western form of state administration. This bureaucratization was a unique historical process which is best understood by comparison with cases where it did not occur, or was much less developed. Weberian historical sociology compares strategic examples in substantial depth, to try to isolate the factors which, in possibly unique combinations, result in the development under investigation. Theoretically guided comparison is pursued to analyse the uniqueness of particular cases. Mouzelis clearly thinks that the (macro) problems of large-scale historical development are the most important, and that their scale and complexity pose the severest test for sociology and social theory. He tries to advance social theory to make this kind of work possible, against contemporary trends which inhibit it (1991: 4). These trends are dominated by the fear of reification and either ignore macro phenomena, or try to derive them from the properties of actors (e.g. rational-choice theory) or face-to-face interaction (e.g. Collins, Knorr-Cetina and Giddens) (Mouzelis 1991: 67–98, 1995: 15–40).

As one might expect, respect for social wholes and their unique historical contexts are central to Mouzelis's own historical sociology in *Modern Greece* (1978) and *Politics in the Semi-periphery* (1986). These studies also reinforce claims for the irreducibility of inequality, hierarchies and the relative autonomy of political techniques of domination. Greek development is shown to involve extreme inequalities, very powerful elites, the highly personalized relations of domination typical of 'clientism', a state which has inhibited autonomous civil society, and vulnerability to military dictatorship. The role of coercion and of powerful institutions (principally the state, army and powerful families) and the actors who direct them from the highest positions is conspicuous. (Mouzelis 1978, 1986). Faced with such a glaring case, Mouzelis finds Lockwood's recommendation and revision of Marxism attractive. Marxism does try to relate system relations (modes of production) to social relations between people (classes). The fate of systems is partly in actors' hands. But Marxism only covers the system of economic production and reduces everything to that, thus failing to provide the 'conceptual tools' needed to analyse a case like Greece, where the political is substantially autonomous from the economic (Mouzelis 1978: xii, 53, 1986: 214–16). Mouzelis tries to extend the analysis of modes of production to the production of political domination as well as economic returns – goods, wages, profits etc., advocating a rapprochement between Marx's political economy and Weber's political sociology (Mouzelis 1986: 199–218).

However, extending the scope of systems analysis to avoid economistic reductionism can do no more than provide the concepts needed to analyse the 'past and present socio-cultural context in which social phenomena are embedded' (Mouzelis 1978: 70). Any non-reified, non-structuralist sociology has to take seriously not only this embeddedness, but the contributions of particular actors to outcomes. So, for example, Greece's unique past as a component of the Ottoman Empire has a significant impact on the continuing domination of civil society by the state. Class relations cannot be understood without acknowledging Greece's location as part of the Balkans subject to western imperialism. The strong institutionalization of local, rural, patron–client relations explains why a strong peasant parliamentary party did not develop (1986: 76–82).

Mouzelis's account is full of such suggestions about how the past shapes the present, and ultimately explains why the 1967 coup occurred. Here the role of factions of army officers, making important decisions about whether and when to act, was crucial. It was the junior officers who seized the initiative from the senior officers (Mouzelis 1978: 132–3). But it could have been different, if the particular actors had been different. While structuralist sociology is uninterested in the specificities of 'who' and 'when', Mouzelis believes sociology must take 'unique historical trajectories' seriously, seeing them as outcomes of the complex 'games' played by actors with the power to make a difference to their structuration.

**The critique of contemporary sociological theory:
the micro–macro relation**

We are now better placed to appreciate why Mouzelis feels something has gone wrong with theory development and that we need to go 'back to sociological theory' (Mouzelis 1991, 1995). Unlike Archer and Giddens, he talks of 'sociological theory' rather than 'social theory' because he wants to assert the autonomy of sociology as a practice quite distinct from other disciplines and particularly philosophy. He thinks it unnecessary to offer extensive philosophical justification for his approach, avoiding, for example, Archer's involvement with philosophical realism and ontological arguments about the nature of human subjectivity (Mouzelis, 1991: 10–22). Mouzelis believes the mark of sociology is empirical investigation and the criterion for theory development the production of a useful 'conceptual tool kit'. He feels that some of the tools existed before the 1960s fragmentation, so that a reconsideration of Parsons is overdue, particularly as the phenomenologists' and interactionists' critique of reification produced a 'micro' sociology offering no tools for dealing with traditional historical sociology's macro problems. As he puts it,

> The task for sociological theory is not one of 'transcendence', of looking *à tout prix* for the uncompromisingly and totally 'new'; neither is it to imperialistically impose the logic (subjectivist or objectivist) of one paradigm ... the task is ... to build bridges between paradigms, to enhance communication between theoretical approaches, so that compartmentalisation is destroyed without at the same time destroying the autonomous logic of existing paradigms.
>
> (Mouzelis 1995: 114)

Thus Mouzelis advocates a modest synthetic dialogue between micro and macro approaches, and builds in particular on Marxism and Parsonian functionalism to provide a 'macro' tool kit that avoids reification.

The so-called 'micro–macro problem' is shorthand for a number of closely related problems which it elides under the difference of 'level' or scale. In particular this elision encourages treating the qualitative differences of kind between social integration (interaction and relations between people) and system integration (relations between institutional elements) as a quantitative difference. Both Mouzelis and Giddens object to treating the macro as an aggregate of the micro as their respective critiques of Collins makes clear (Giddens 1984: 140–2; Mouzelis 1991: 80–8, 1995: 22–5). Giddens wants to get rid of the micro–macro distinction because it dualistically associates 'structure' with the macro, and agency with the micro. We saw him seeking to install structure within agency and interaction (the micro) while allowing for the variable distanciation of agency/structure (the macro). Mouzelis, on the other hand, regards the micro–macro distinction as useful, provided it refers to differences in the scope and power of the agency of actors, and is clearly separated from the distinction between social and system integration. The *micro–macro dimension is best thought of as one of continuous quantitative variation of the power of actors to exercise more or less extensive influence* over other people's lives, whereas the social integration – systems integration distinction refers to a difference of kind. Here Mouzelis plays his social theoretical trump card, 'hierarchization', to enable the two kinds of distinction to be related to one another.

Social hierarchies, rules and games

The concept of hierarchy (see Figure 7.1) does a huge amount of work for Mouzelis and is the most generally useful item in his tool kit. This is because it specifies a mode of relation which applies to the *components of institutions* (rules and roles, i.e. systems integration), the *participants* in interaction (role incumbents and collective actors, i.e. social integration) and *variability* of agency and constraint. We have seen how institutions are relatively fixed, organized hierarchical orders of roles and rules, with power implications for the actors who occupy positions in them. One of the most important properties of hierarchies is *the relative autonomy*

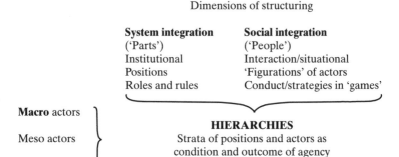

Figure 7.1   Hierarchies relate micro to macro and system to social integration

of levels: 'The notion of the hierarchisation of social systems implies that subordinate systems . . . portray varying degrees of autonomy (that is "boundedness") *vis-à-vis* superordinate ones' (Mouzelis 1995: 168). Relative autonomy applies to subsystems, such as departments of organizations, and roles within them occupied by actors. All levels have their specific emergent properties which confer on actors at least *some* powers of agency. Where subordinate subsystems and actors have zero autonomy, 'we can no longer speak of social system hierarchisation'. (Thus it is possible to argue that those right at the bottom of hierarchies derive no benefit from their position since it is not until one moves up at least one level that any emergence can take place.) So it is relations of super- and subordination which determine the *degrees of agency and constraint* attaching to the various levels at which actors operate – micro, meso and macro. This is a non-reified conceptualizing of structural constraint since it flows from being positioned in relations with other actors whose powers are different from one's own. What constrains, socially speaking, is relations with the other, hierarchically positioned, actors with whom one interacts.

Institutions supply the 'positional', or 'systemic' dimension of social life, but positions must be realized interactionally. Thus, in the 'social integration' dimension of social life, participants, actual interacting people, individually and collectively, using the potentialities of their positions, struggle to maintain or improve their relative standing in 'games'. Mouzelis, like Bourdieu, speaks of people as playing social 'games', strategically using rules to 'play' (that is cooperate and compete) effectively. So positions in institutional hierarchies do not automatically determine outcomes; the 'high-ups' do not automatically win every game, unless their skill and luck encountering contingencies are also favourable. However, Mouzelis resists the reproductive bias of Bourdieu's approach (which elides position and disposition) by insisting on the irreducibility of the 'interactional–situational' dimension of games (Mouzelis 1995: 110). The actual course of struggles or games has a relative autonomy such that results may be at odds with what might be expected, knowing the initial distribution of power and dispositions among the competitors. The weak can be skilful and/or lucky, and the strong can squander their advantages. The relation between actors and structures is therefore far from mechanical and determined; how agency is manifested in the way games are played contributes to ensuring history is open and unpredictable. The analysis of games, therefore, necessarily involves relations between *positional, dispositional and interactional/situational* factors whose significance varies between cases (Mouzelis 1995: 108). And it is as outcomes of games that the maintenance, or transformation, of relations of relative advantage and disadvantage, and the 'figuration' (Elias) of alliances and compromises among participants, are to be explained.

Thinking of structures as institutional and figurational hierarchies allows them to be conditions of agency, and for agency, in the form of participation in cooperative and competitive games, to reproduce or transform structural hierarchies. The mutual interdependence of structure and agency in the process of structuration is established, but in a relation of non-identity, mediated by eventfull histories of actual interaction between micro, meso and macroactors. Though Mouzelis does not emphasize the temporal element, the resemblance to Archer's position is evident.

The restructuring of 'structuration' theory

Mouzelis builds his tool kit by synthesizing parts of the work of those he criticizes. We have just seen him taking elements from Bourdieu and Elias. The following sections show how he draws on Giddens and then Parsons and Marx.

Paradigmatic and syntagmatic dimensions of structure

Mouzelis believes that actors can orientate to structures, the given elements of their social environments, in various ways depending on their institutional (systems, rules, the *de jure*) and figurational (social, games, the *de facto*) location. In his critique of Giddens he uses structural linguistic's distinction between the *paradigmatic and syntagmatic dimensions of structuring* to develop his point (Mouzelis 1991: 25–47, 1995: 117–26). A paradigm defines the rules governing the use of, say, parts of speech. Such rules are only virtual because they define only conditions of possibility and do not describe or determine any particular, concrete, historical utterance. The syntagm is the actual sequences produced by mobilizing the paradigmatic rules. Here the relation is not one of systematic vertical substitution, but of horizontal location in a temporal sequence. The syntagm describes the specific order of events, which in the case of social phenomena are actual histories of interaction and the emergence of reproductive or transformative outcomes.

Relating structure and agency: dualism and duality

Mouzelis asserts, against Giddens, that structures are only partly virtual. They entail both the paradigmatic potentialities of 'rules and resources' existing as virtual realities and the realized, syntagmatic dimension. Mouzelis does not, as Healy suggests, leave Giddens's definition of structure 'largely untouched', but rather adds the syntagmatic dimension to it (Healy 1998: 509). This partial acceptance is then extended to Giddens's assertion that structure and agency relate as a duality. Mouzelis agrees that agents commonly relate to the paradigmatic conditions of their action in a taken-for-granted, routine fashion, using their practical consciousness and knowledgeability, with possibly recursive consequences. He accepts that structure can be the 'medium and outcome' of agency. But he insists that actors, equally commonly, do not relate to paradigmatic rules and resources in a taken-for-granted fashion. They can dualistically 'distance' themselves from the rules, relating to them in a contemplative, theoretical and/or strategic fashion (Mouzelis 1991: 27–30). This distancing from the taken-for-granted is typical of self-reflexive human beings (Mouzelis invokes G.H. Mead; 1995: 136) but is encouraged by collective action to defend or change existing institutions and rules, and by the experience of discrepancies between expectations and outcomes (Mouzelis 1995: 139–40). In other words, humans are typically critics as well as followers of routines, their structure-manipulating and theorizing capacity contributing to the structuration of history. Mouzelis

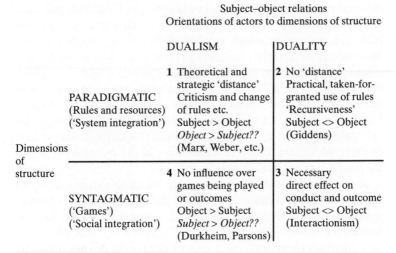

Subject–object relations
Orientations of actors to dimensions of structure

		DUALISM	DUALITY
Dimensions of structure	PARADIGMATIC (Rules and resources) ('System integration')	**1** Theoretical and strategic 'distance' Criticism and change of rules etc. Subject > Object *Object > Subject??* (Marx, Weber, etc.)	**2** No 'distance' Practical, taken-for-granted use of rules 'Recursiveness' Subject <> Object (Giddens)
	SYNTAGMATIC ('Games') ('Social integration')	**4** No influence over games being played or outcomes Object > Subject *Subject > Object??* (Durkheim, Parsons)	**3** Necessary direct effect on conduct and outcome Subject <> Object (Interactionism)

Figure 7.2 The restructuring of 'structuration' theory

rejects Giddens's reduction of the structure–agency dualism to duality, just as he rejects his reduction of the syntagmatic to the paradigmatic.

Mouzelis's restructuring of 'structuration' theory therefore involves relating the difference between the paradigmatic *and* syntagmatic dimensions of structure to agency–structure relations of dualism *and* duality. He wants to enable 'structuration' theory to recognize the variability of social constraint and powers of agency, characteristic of positions in hierarchies, making it useful for substantive empirical analysis. But his tendency to describe and illustrate his theoretical scheme in terms of positions in hierarchies can be a source of confusion (Healy 1998). It is better, initially, not to follow him too closely, but to describe the analytical logic in a 'hierarchy-neutral' way to bring out certain implicit elements. This is attempted in Figure 7.2 and my discussion below.

Box 2 shows Mouzelis's acceptance of the possibility of duality at the paradigmatic level. Here, with Giddens, he sees structure and agency, subject and object, as 'internally' related – there is no 'distance' between them. Box 1 depicts paradigmatic dualism where there can be a 'distance', or external relation, between structure and agency, acknowledging that agents can reject, criticize and innovate rules, rather than simply follow them. However, the external relation of dualism is a two-way street. Collective and individual macro-actors can determine rules (Subject>Objects) and rules can determine actors (*Object>Subjects*). As Archer shows, there are good grounds for seeing rules, *qua* rules, as having the relative autonomy of logic – which is a source of structural constraint bearing equally on all. But Mouzelis only ever talks about the subject-to-object mode of relation. So the logic of his theorizing is good, but his exposition incomplete. While three relations are logically implied, only two are actually described, one variant of external dualism (Subject>Objects), and the mutuality of internal duality (Subjects<>Objects).

This oversight probably results from Mouzelis's strong desire to create a conceptual space where social theory can recognize macro-actors' agency with respect to rules and institutions. Though he abhors the reduction of the objective realities of social structures and criticizes those who overreact to the threat of reification, he seems to do this himself. Hence his failing to consider, in his account of paradigmatic dualism, the objective autonomy of rules and the kinds of constraint they can exercise independently of actors' power (*Object>Subject*).

Similar problems arise with regard to syntagmatic subject–object relations. Again taking his cue from Giddens and the interactionists, Mouzelis describes syntagmatic duality (Box 3) as a relation of constitutive necessity between participants and the conduct of games. It is the relation between producers of outcomes who are also affected by them, as winners or losers perhaps. This is the box where actors show their strategic skills at games playing and the interactional elements of structure are internal to agency. Initially this seems reasonable, but, as Healy indicates, it conflates all the different ways in which actors are 'necessary' for the conduct of games. Mouzelis emphasizes the necessity of 'copresence' in interaction situations, but macro-actors, in particular, can influence games in their absence. In general Mouzelis insists actors make 'asymmetrical differential contributions' to outcomes, because some have more extensive and effective powers than others, so an element of dualism must creep in to the games playing of syntagmatic duality. Interactionist micro-sociology has never adequately acknowledged differences of power.

This issue of power is central to Mouzelis's depiction of syntagmatic dualism (Box 4) which, as with his discussion of paradigmatic dualism, has a one-sided emphasis, this time on the structural determination of agency. Mouzelis wants to allow for cases where subjects are external to the games being played because they have virtually no influence over them or their outcomes. He speaks of syntagmatic dualism as pertaining 'to a situation where subjects rightly perceive structural properties as external, in the sense that as single actors, they have neither contributed significantly to their reproduction, nor can they transform them without radically changing their present power position' (Mouzelis 1991: 39). But this sort of relation needs to be matched by its opposite, the unopposed voluntarism of the ultra-powerful. Where should we place Caligula, or the German army in the Warsaw Ghetto? Syntagmatic dualism in the *Subject>Object* variant seems more appropriate than the soft voluntarism of syntagmatic duality, implied by Mouzelis's exposition.

Perhaps the duality/dualism distinction at the syntagmatic level is not very helpful if, as we have seen, elements of dualism are involved in syntagmatic duality, and syntagmatic dualism should include both Object>Subject and *Subject>Object* possibilities. At the syntagmatic level Mouzelis uses 'dualism' to refer to the determination of subjects by social objects, and 'duality' to refer to the opposite variant of the dualistic relation. Clearly the theorizing is driven by a sense of the irreducibility of dualism to allow social theory to deal with the variability in the force of structure and agency in actual historical cases. But to retain the term 'duality' to refer to the subject-dominant variant of dualism is perhaps rather generous to Giddens. What is at issue is whether, at the syntagmatic level of games playing, there is anything analogous to the 'recursiveness' which just might be plausibly claimed for the paradigmatic level of practical rule use. Given the openness of the outcomes of games and uncertainty about their reproductive and transforming consequences for hierarchies, we must ask *what can be described by syntagmatic duality which cannot be described by syntagmatic dualism, once both variants (subject>object and object>subject) are included*?

Taking tennis, we might, for the sake of argument, accept that every actual match, by following the institutionalized rules of 'the game of tennis', contributes recursively to tennis's reproduction (paradigmatic duality). But the actual playing of each game is an historically unique sequence of shots, movements and scoring, as advantage flows back and forth between the players, ending in a result. The play cannot logically be reproducing itself since it is only

Paradigmatic (Virtual elements of structure)	**Dualism (i)** Actors criticize & create rules ('distance')	**Dualism (ii)** Autonomy of logic of rules	**Duality** Routine use of rules: recursiveness (no 'distance')
Syntagmatic (Concrete elements of structure)	**Dualism (i)** Actors have power to affect outcomes of games	**Dualism (ii)** Actors have no power to affect outcomes of games	???

Figure 7.3 A restructuring of Mouzelis's restructuring of 'structuration' theory

revealed as the play proceeds; after all it is play, not the rules for play. But the results of games do have reproductive and trans-formative implications for the standing of the players, promoting or demoting them in the syntagmatic figurations of tennis-related 'rankings' (hierarchies). These outcomes are explained by differences in the powers of agents as tennis players and how difficult they find playing generally and their opponents in particular games – exactly what syntagmatic dualism covers analytically.

This appraisal suggests that Mouzelis's argument establishes the need for dualism, but not the extension of duality to the syntagmatic level. The alternative implicit in his thinking is represented in Figure 7.3.

Mouzelis rightly insists that hierarchized social orders require recognizing dualism's irreducibility. But once Lockwood's distinction between social and system integration (as the paradigm/syntagm distinction) is rescued from Giddens's redefinition of it, and the full range of possibilities implied by dualism is recognized, enough logical space is created for a social theory capable of handling hierarchized structures without reification. *If* there is a place for duality, it is only at the paradigmatic level which Giddens originally proposed. There seems to be no work for a concept of syntagmatic duality to do.

The defence of functional analysis; synthesizing Marx and Parsons

Mouzelis provides tools for analysing social games played by hier-archized actors, micro, meso and macro, whose outcomes are the result of the interaction of positional, dispositional and inter-actional/situational factors. The dualism of structure and agency allows for the variability of agentic powers and structural constraint typical of hierarchies. The relative autonomy of levels, roles, their incumbents, and the specific situations of interaction is maintained. To complete this very useful kit Mouzelis develops tools for analysing institutions and systems by combining analytical principles from Marx and Parsons. Each has a major weakness: 'if various forms of economic reductionism have been and remain the Achilles' heel of all Marxism, the inadequate conceptualisation of collective action and its articulation with the institutional structures of complex societies is the basic flaw in both Parsonian functionalism and of interpretive sociologies' (Mouzelis 1991: 60). However, Marx's economism can be countered by Parsons's functional prerequisites, and Parsons's reification of systems by Marx's analysis of the social and systems integration of modes of production.

First, Mouzelis thinks Parsons's four functional prerequisites of the continued functioning of social systems define the *necessary conditions* of existence for institutions and organizations. Collectivities such as businesses or schools have 'needs' for resources (Adaptation), effective leadership (Goal attainment), organization and motivation of personnel (Integration), and some orientation to cultural values (Latency) (Mouzelis 1995: 131–2). But necessary conditions are not sufficient to explain actual institutions. Conditions have to be acted upon. The only 'sufficient causation' in social reality is the active pursuit of interests by collective actors participating in divisions of labour and hierarchies (p. 133). Mouzelis sees Parsons's succumbing to reification when he attributes system needs to abstractions such as 'the economy', or to subsystems emerging to satisfy particular functional prerequisites. Reification is unavoidable if subsystems are not considered as organized actors pursuing collective ends (like departments of an organization), but as systems in their own right dependent on their own AGIL necessities, which in turn generate sub-subsystems ad infinitum (pp. 87–90). Only collectivities have functional needs and the actors to supply them. Parsons mistook *necessary conditions* for *sufficient causes*. But he is valuable for countering Marx's economic determinism with a Weberian recognition that *collective organization depends equally on economic, political and cultural conditions.* We are reminded of Mouzelis's frustration with Marxism for analysing Greek culture and politics.

	Parsons's functional prerequisites: AGIL Adaptation + Goal attainment + Integration + Latency		
Institutional spheres: **Economic**	**Political**		**Cultural**
Marx: Forces of production +	**Technologies** of economic,	political, and	cultural production
Relations of production +	**Appropriation** of economic,	political, and	cultural production
Ideology	**Ideology** (legitimation) of the relations of economic, political and cultural production and appropriation		

Figure 7.4   The synthesis of Parsons and Marx for the analysis of institutions in terms of social and system integration

Parsons's AGIL schema suggests why there are the institutions there are, and Marx's concept of a mode of production, extended from the economic to cultural and political spheres, suggests how institutional parts and actors relate within them (Mouzelis 1995: 90–2). Marx links institutional or system relations to the social relations of actors using the concepts of forces and relations of production, which Mouzelis calls resource-producing *'technologies'* and relations of *'appropriation'*. The third concept, *'ideology'*, refers to the legitimation of the relations of appropriation. Mouzelis sees production, appropriation and ideology as fundamental to analysis of relations between the different sorts of institutional hierarchies and games collective actors participate in, which are the objects of institutional analysis. His elegant synthesis is shown in Figure 7.4.

The use of Marxian concepts to subdivide each institutional sphere links institutional wholes to actors' cooperating and conflictual relationships. The functional analysis of the prerequisites of institutions' existence is pursued through examining the way actors relate in order to produce and appropriate economic, political and cultural resources or 'capital' (Mouzelis 1995: 90–2, 146). Mouzelis places inequalities and conflicts about who appropriates and controls the various technologies and the use of resources at the heart of functional analysis. These 'structural cleavages' help answer, in terms of the state of system integration, questions about who suffers, gains, decides etc. Combining Marx's and Parsons's institutional analyses yields a much more sophisticated basis for analysing system integration and the sources of incompatibilities which divide or hierarchize actors (pp. 95–8). The synthesis allows relations between institutional parts to be articulated with actors' strategies and struggles, which is precluded by Parsons's over-systemic reifying approach.

Mouzelis thus completes his tool kit for analysing social games and players. Parsons's ideas about necessary conditions of exist-ence of organized collectivities are linked to Marx's understanding of the social relations involved in producing these necessities. The objective requirements of enduring organizations and the objective relations entailed by productive agency – divisions of labour, relations of appropriation, economic, political and cultural hierar-chization – are given equal weight. These are what social games are necessarily about (Mouzelis 1995: 151). As for the players, this formula for institutional analysis allows the identification of real, non-teleological mechanisms of structuration and development. These are the collectivities (e.g. classes, quasi-groups) which exer-cise agency through the interaction of micro, meso and macro decision makers (elites, leaders, representatives) in the conduct of games. Systems do not 'do' anything; actors (collective and indi-vidual) do. So, Mouzelis advises beginning analysis of macro developments by identifying the relevant hierarchies and (collec-tive or individual) macro-actors who have the decision-making power to influence macro change (Mouzelis 1991: 117–18, 1995: 136–8). Social theory which cannot recognize the importance of a Stalin, Churchill or Roosevelt on the world historical stage, as well as a General Motors, Oxfam or NATO, is useless (Mouzelis 1991: 82–3). The hierarchical variability of agency allows that *some* actors, because they are collectivities and/or by virtue of their pos-itions in hierarchies, *may* have macroscopic powers. This permits social wholes to be analysed in a non-reified way, and avoids the reductionism and utopian voluntarism of micro-sociology. The agency capable of structuring institutions and games is itself con-strained and enabled by pre-existing hierarchized positions within such institutions and games (Mouzelis 1995: 128–9). Structure and agency are thus interdependent, balanced elements of historical structuration.

8

The Recovery of History and Structure

Introduction

The purpose of this chapter is to review the alternatives offered by Bourdieu, Giddens, Archer and Mouzelis. Chapters 4–7 focused on the differences between 'structurationists' and post-'structurationists' with regard to the question of the identity (duality) or non-identity (dualism) of structure and agency, deliberately emphasizing the major cleavage between the two groups of theorists. However, that Bourdieu and Giddens virtually ignore one another, that Archer opposes herself so uncompromisingly to Giddens (but less emphatically to Bourdieu) while ignoring Mouzelis, that Mouzelis himself makes only passing reference to Archer while drawing substantially on Bourdieu and Giddens, suggests there are issues which cross-cut the major cleavage over the structure–agency relation. This chapter will describe this pattern of similarities and differences.

Fundamental agreement about the basic problem

Whatever their differences, all the theorists are fundamentally committed to avoiding objectivism and subjectivism in social theory. All try to show how subject and object are related as equally essential elements in the structuration process. All are opposed to the reification of social systems, and the teleological understanding of historical development. They defend human agency as the only 'sufficient causation' in history. Conversely, all reject reduction of the objectivity of structures to subjectivity of agents, typical of individualism, interactionism and 'micro-sociology' generally. Structures constrain agency and extravagant voluntarism is rejected. All therefore offer ways through the reification–reduction impasse by conceptualizing structures as constraining the agency which produces them. But, as Chapter 1 noted, the arguments are about *how*, not whether, structure and agency are related.

The 'structurationist' solution: practice

Bourdieu and Giddens connect them by concentrating on a point in the structuration process – 'practice' – where both structure and agency are empirically and experientially indistinguishable. The concept of practice establishes the duality, or identity, of structure and agency. Structure is realized as it is used to enable agency. The relation is forged, moment by moment, in the ongoing 'doing' of agents. Practice is a 'process' concept which enables structure and agency to constitute each other simultaneously. As Bourdieu puts it, 'practice is inseparable from temporality' (1990b: 81). But as Archer points out, this temporality is highly compressed, as the relation is made and remade in the immediate present, as actors show they 'know how to carry on' (Giddens) and respond to the 'urgency of practice' (Bourdieu). The concept of practice dictates that the structure–agency relation will be one of 'instantiation', lacking historical depth. Past and future are collapsed into the present to achieve the desired 'balanced synthesis'.

The imperative character of practice restricts reflectiveness and taking time to choose, raising 'practical consciousness' (Giddens) and 'habitus' (Bourdieu) above rational deliberation in human action. Concentration on what could be called the urgency of the present forces reliance on habituated responses and dispositions. This restricts agents to the relatively limited power to contribute to the reproduction of established tendencies, patterns of distribution and routines 'recursively'. Thus voluntaristic pretensions for agency are trimmed into a sufficiently non-heroic form to allow it to be identified with structure. Similarly, the concept of practice restricts the force of structure to its contribution to the conduct of moments of practice.

Agency is reduced by either relatively *weakening* or *strengthening* structure. Giddens weakens structure so that the process of practical enactment in interaction displaces consideration of how structural constraint endures, whatever agents do. Enduring, non-momentary structural constraint is rendered insubstantial as Giddens recognizes by deeming structures to be only virtual, elements of actors' *knowledge*, when not being instantiated. Moreover their capacity to constrain agency must be logically identical with their capacity to enable it. Thus 'dissolving social structure into social action removes the object of social action: it can only act upon itself, not upon social structures' (Craib 1986: 19). The claim that humans are capable of historical agency is undermined by virtually removing what they may be up against when trying to transform structures.

Bourdieu opts to strengthen structure by conceptualizing it as the distribution of scarce resources required to engage in practice. Structure is strengthened relative to agency, though reduced to only a hierarchical distributional order of power. This dissolves social action into its structural conditions. Instead of virtualizing structure, Bourdieu almost virtualizes agency. This follows from retaining the conventional understanding of social structure as differentiated positions, while trying to unite structure and agency via practice. Bourdieu argues that the past, in the form of structural conditions, casts a long shadow over the present *and* that the present moment of practice is autonomous. But unless structure is virtualized, or agency exaggerated, agency will tend to be absorbed by its structural preconditions and become little more than a reflection of *power*. Giddens sees that to identify structure with agency, structure must be virtualized. But his structuration theory thereby becomes inconsistent with his substantive historical sociology where non-virtual properties of social structures return with a vengeance. Conversely, Bourdieu maintains an important element of sociological realism, though his refusal to virtualize structure (or inflate agency) while relating structure and agency via practice is theoretically inconsistent. Giddens is the more consistent theorist, Bourdieu the better sociologist.

Using the concept of practice to escape the reification–reduction impasse involves trimming structure (by virtualizing it, or reducing it to hierarchies of power) and agency (by reducing its object or by making it dependent on its conditions). Subject and object are related by reducing what is claimed for each. Practice links structure and agency securely in the tightest of relations, that of identity. But for this relation and moment to be sufficient to constitute society, the durability and substantial autonomy of structures and agents must be denied. 'Structurationists' are driven by their sense of what constitutes a convincing form of relation between the two. Given social theory's polarization between objectivism and subjectivism, perhaps they felt that claiming the identity of structure and agency was rhetorically required. But establishing a practice-based relation of identity involved paying a high price in reduction. Relying on the present instant of practice allows a universal, constant and timeless logical relation of identity to be asserted. This satisfies utopian aspirations, but diverts attention from the other, non-logical kinds of variable and contingent relations, which appear when one places the present within the wider temporal perspective of history.

Major differences between Giddens and Bourdieu: position, power and interests

Though Bourdieu and Giddens use practice to identify structure with agency, there is a substantial difference in how they conceptualize power and interests and the weight they attach to the positional dimension of social life, which affects how they account for structuration. Since both hard-headedly oppose voluntaristic subjectivism, they must deal with the issue of power in social life. We have seen how Bourdieu's disenchantment sets practice in contexts of power structures. His conventional sociological approach to power locates agents in the pre-existing hierarchies of competitive fields from which their social power and collective interests derive. Position and disposition are so tightly combined that person and social self become indistinguishable. Persons pursue objectively structured collective interests informed by their habitus in a highly predictable and predominantly reproductive fashion. This limits the scope for innovation or acting against type, and is Bourdieu's version of Parsons's 'scientifically relevant subjective aspect' (Parsons [1937]1968: 46).

Giddens, on the other hand, has to theorize power without any positional concept of structure within which to locate actors. As Mouzelis and Archer point out, Giddens's version of social reality is essentially 'flat'. He cannot derive power or interests from positional differences of the hierarchical sort Bourdieu favours. Instead he makes two moves. First, he attributes power as an existential principle of the humanity of agents, irrespective of position. No one is without power in the 'dialectic of control'. Interests are generalized from the various 'needs' of individuals, primarily for 'ontological security'. This universalizing of positionless power and interest at the analytical level of the individual parallels methodological individualism's and utilitarianism's attempt to derive agency from the innate characteristics of 'human nature'. Giddens makes his second move in his account of social systems development – a story of progressive distanciation which implies that everyone has a general interest in time–space extension. Again, this is a general, positionless interest which provides no basis for explaining systematic social conflict. As for power itself, Giddens's historical sociology makes its bid for realism by pointing to relations between different kinds of power – economic, ideological and, above all, military/coercive. Giddens is eventually strung out between the utopian universality of human capacity for agency and the realist rhetoric of the ever-present threat of violence.

The contrast is stark; Bourdieu derives differences of power and interests solely from positional structures, while Giddens derives them solely from individual human persons. Giddens therefore, since he lacks any concepts of social structures as specific kinds of relations between collectivities, is the only thinker discussed in this book who has *no concept of the collective basis of agency*. Even in the *ad hoc* realm of his historical sociology, structures only collectivize by 'binding' the time and space of interaction into more or less distanciated regions. These are systems only in the sense of exhibiting regularities in the virtual structures used by agents to interact, rather than relations between systematically reproduced and differentiated collectivities. Giddens's 'structuration' theory therefore has no access to collective agency and power exercised through struggles, as a mechanism for explaining the structuration of what he calls systems. The theory cannot identify collective agents or analyse social integration in terms of relations between collectivities. Indeed, this problem of finding collective agents continues into his more recent analysis of radical politics which concludes with the vague utopian claim that as we enter a 'post-scarcity order', 'We are now in a world where there are *many* others; but also one where there *are* no others' (Giddens 1994: 253).

Bourdieu's acknowledgement of the effect of distributional structures on agency, power and interests, on the other hand, allows him to give a sort of answer to the 'who' questions. It forms the bridge to Archer and Mouzelis's dualist, post-'structurationist' position.

But not much can travel across it because agency, conditioned by a habitus reflecting the current distributional order, *biases practice towards inertia* and hence the structure's reproduction. The past drives agency because habitus and the urgency of practice together impose pressures which make it difficult for practice to escape being reproductive. This positional/dispositional conditioning of practice overwhelms consideration of the sources of non-reproductive emergence such as the relations between autonomous practices, the historical specificity of institutional contexts, the contradictions and contingencies of situations, the effectiveness of collective mobilization, and the distinctiveness of individual agents.

Relating structure and agency through the concept of practice entails the unification and homogenization of the historical process of structuration. Just as Parsons's teleology presented development as 'a smooth and harmonious process . . . towards greater complexity and adaptive capacity' (Mouzelis 1995: 82), so Giddens and Bourdieu, by emphasizing the 'flow' of the process of 'becoming', also give an impression of smoothness. Though their history is not going anywhere – is not on any developmental track – it might as well be. For Giddens, every 'instantiating' moment is one of unspecifiable change and the unexpected. For Bourdieu, what people do in moments of practice is highly predictable and reproductive. For both, history is therefore all of a piece, just as it is for teleological modernization theorists. Teleologists' 'world-growth story' accounts for the whole of history, whilst 'structurationists' confine themselves to the immediacy of practice. But both neglect the same thing – the realm of historical processes and their products whose *temporality is more enduring than the present and less than the whole of historical time*. Neither can answer 'when' questions.

To escape the ironic similarity of teleology and 'structuration' theory, both 'structurationists' would have to theorize an 'intermediate' temporality, that of relations between specific events and agency. Giddens could perhaps then supply theoretical grounds to account for tendencies (why they start and continue) and limit the unexpected, and Bourdieu might explain the disturbing of tendencies (why they stop and change) and limit the expected. Deepening historical time to encompass relations among events enables finding processes which can produce durable structures, regular patterns of interaction and developmental tendencies with relatively high predictability on the one hand, and volatile, unstable, randomized, quick-changing unpredictability on the other.

The fixation with practice and establishing a relation of identity between structure and agency routinizes agency, but makes it very difficult to distinguish between more and less significant agency for the structuration of historical developments. The moments of practice preclude identifying moments of structuration. Despite their different definitions of structure, Giddens and Bourdieu simply take its existence for granted. The routinization of agency, to avoid reification, paradoxically reduces its capacity to be historically creative *sometimes*. Bourdieu can say 'who' but not 'when' and Giddens can say neither 'who' nor 'when'.

The post-'structurationist' solution: social theory for 'rough' history

We have already seen how Archer and Mouzelis criticize the 'structurationists'. They agree that dualism is necessary and are less critical of Bourdieu than Giddens (though Archer is more hostile than Mouzelis). To put it schematically, whereas Bourdieu and Giddens theorize history as 'smooth', at least Bourdieu recognizes the importance of hierarchies. For Bourdieu, Archer and Mouzelis the social world is certainly not 'flat'! The post-'structurationists'' agreement derives from their practical engagement with a specific kind of macro-sociology. Both have attempted to explain the development of systematic institutional differences between specific societies during specific historical periods. This sort of comparative historical sociology tries to explain institutional development by analysing relatively long time periods, identifying the relations between the relevant competing collective agents, the outcomes of specific events of conflict, the effects of contingencies, and the emergent outcomes of action which cumulatively contribute to the particular institutional tendency being explained. It cannot avoid seeking out the actors and events that matter and specifying the ways these actors and events produce outcomes which change the configuration of forces constraining action, making some future developments more, and others less, likely. Their historical sociology seeks only the wisdom of hindsight.

This practical experience of middle-range macro-sociology provides their criteria for assessing the adequacy of social theory. It must provide the basis for an explanatory method which offers guidance for practical social theorizing about actual cases (Archer) or, in Mouzelis's terms, a 'tool kit'. Both emphasize that social theory must enable the practical analyst to identify with *precision* the historically important agency, structural constraints and their interplay. Only regarding these as analytically distinct creates the theoretical room to establish just who and what contributes to the structuration of the developments under investigation. The 'structurationist' duality formula, conflating structure and agency, cannot be precise about such questions. Central to the post-'structurationist' position is the realization that if agency is to play a part in social analysis it must be conceptualized by reference to the powers which produce specific outcomes. As Archer puts it, 'Social agency is not just a pretentious way of referring to people or humankind' (Archer 1995: 248). Though all human beings may be agents in the sense of having the basic capability to make a difference, what matters for social analysis is what converts that capability into an agency that is historically consequential. Such a sociology depends on being able to conceptualize the relative autonomy of the structures conditioning agency and recognizing that it takes time for the effects of agency to emerge. The recovery of structure and historical time together is necessary.

If objectivism/structuralism (Archer's 'downward conflation') postulates strong structures and weak agents, subjectivism ('upwards conflation') the reverse, and 'structurationists' ('central conflation') weak structures and weak agents, the post-'structurationists' postulate *both* strong and weak agents *and* strong and weak structures. Only with such possibilities can the 'zig-zags', the 'stop–go' (Archer), the 'interrupted' or 'reversible' (Mouzelis) developments typical of a 'rough' history, be analysed, and the utopian smoothness of teleological inevitability or a flowing instantiation be avoided.

The differences between Archer and Mouzelis: time and hierarchy

Despite basic agreement about what practical social theorizing involves, there are substantial differences in Archer's and Mouzelis's social ontology and explanatory methodology. These follow from Archer's basing herself in the kind of philosophical debates about social reality and subjectivity which Mouzelis feels should be bypassed to get 'back to sociological theory' (Mouzelis 1991: 10–24). This is their fundamental disagreement, though one suspects that Mouzelis could concur with Archer's philosophical conclusions. Nonetheless, there are important differences of emphasis in how they build on Lockwood's fundamental distinction between social and system integration. They obviously vary in the dimensions they choose to identify the variable but undissolvable relation between structure and agency. For Archer it is *time*, for Mouzelis, *hierarchy*. The significance of this is shown by contrasting their treatments of structures, emergence, the relative autonomy of levels, the structural conditioning of agency, and actors.

For Archer, structure includes anything which pre-exists agency, has durability and relative autonomy, is causally efficacious and may be elaborated in interaction. Structures are the outcomes of past agency. Temporality is a fundamental condition of structures' existence. Structures emerge over time to become relatively autonomous, durable conditions of action. Agency is conditioned by anything which has emerged with sufficient autonomy to exercise constraint. That must include Mouzelis's institutional and figurational hierarchies and the positions of particular individuals and collectivities within them. But Archer bases her concept of structure in realist ontology so that the relative autonomy of levels refers to emergent levels of reality where specific kinds of causal power start to operate, whereas Mouzelis's structured levels are those in social hierarchies which distribute power to actors. Unlike Archer, he acknowledges no emergent differences of kind. Mouzelis's levels are of *one* kind – hierarchies; Archer's are of *kinds*.

Archer's approach can recognize any kind of emergent constraint conditioning action. Mouzelis, by contrast, concentrates on the undoubtedly very important condition of hierarchical positions. This does not contradict Archer's relating of structure and agency using time, since hierarchies satisfy her criteria for structures – they pre-exist agency, condition it and are elaborated by it. Mouzelis's social games take time to play and yield results, but what emerges are redistributions and repositionings, not differences of kind. Despite criticizing Bourdieu's underplaying of the 'interactional/situational' dimension of games, Mouzelis, with Bourdieu, reduces the autonomy of practices to players' gains and losses of capitals or power. This loses sources of differences and relations which do not arise from differences of power or hierarchies (Crowther 1994).

Hierarchy does establish the interdependence and variability of the powers of structure and agency. It allows that actors differ in their contributions to outcomes and are unequally constrained. Actors can be sorted into those whose agency does and does not count. Dualism is required. Temporality is integral to the process. Who and when can be determined. Events happen, contingency intervenes, and there are products of the process. But hierarchical conditioning and repositioning is a rather abbreviated vision of the historical process of structuration. For Mouzelis the outcomes of games are open – history is indeed 'rough' (in both senses). But he uses Parsons and Marx to say what the games are always about – producing and appropriating the economic, political and cultural capitals of each institutional sphere. This formula is not wrong but is so general that it does not help to detect kinds of emergent, constraining structures which are not distributive outcomes. Mouzelis's method of theoretical synthesis perhaps inhibits him from breaking free from his functionalist and Marxist sources.

Mouzelis's autonomy of practices is not the autonomy of their specific character but only of the function which they contribute to satisfying. Almost certainly, despite rejecting systems functionalism, Archer would agree with Mouzelis that collectivities have functional needs they must meet if they are to operate to secure their ends. But she would regard this as a truism and no substitute for closely specifying the relations between actual practices in specific historical situations to determine the conditioning of agency which results in emergence and structuration. Both she and Mouzelis agree that there is no substitute for painstaking detailed analysis of the historical situations in which outcomes emerge.

Situational analysis, structurally conditioned agency, and the autonomy of persons

Archer's social theory is the more sophisticated not because it has a superior view of what the analysis of structuration involves, but because she takes less for granted than Mouzelis who leaves *'situations'* and *'people'* under-theorized.

I doubt Mouzelis would object to anything in Archer's specification of what is involved in the situational analysis demanded by the non-teleological, non-'instantiating', historico-genetic narratives both approve of. His own rule of thumb, to start by identifying the macro-actors with the power to influence macro outcomes, is fine as far as it goes. But Archer's achievement is to make explicit the systematic set of relations for analysing the four logics of situations (compromise, elimination, protection and opportunism) (see Figure 6.2). These guide the practical analyst to identify the socially structured agency ('social integration') manifested in the opportunity-cost calculations of vested interests, and the necessary and contingent contradictions and complementarities among emergent cultural and structural properties ('systems integration'). Mouzelis could easily recognize this as a description of his actual practice when analysing the structuration of the unique trajectory of Greek political and economic development (Mouzelis 1978).

Similarly, where Mouzelis talks straightforwardly about actors, distinguished only by hierarchical level (micro, meso, macro), Archer analytically distinguishes between social agents (primary and corporate), actors and persons. Mouzelis assumes the capacity of actors for agency, subject only to their hierarchical position (in the manner of Bourdieu). Their dispositions, interests and strategic orientation are structurally conditioned, and their capacity for strategic games playing taken for granted. The structurally conditioned tendencies which are set in play, variations in strategic skill, and contingencies, explain the variability of outcomes. Most telling, the claim that actors can reflectively 'distance' themselves from the paradigmatic rules, so crucial to his defence of dualism against Giddens, remains unjustified (see Figure 7.2).

Archer theorizes the constitution of agency more thoroughly. Consistent with her analytical realism, she carefully distinguishes the levels at which relatively autonomous properties emerge which establish the capability to contribute to structuration. People are involuntarily placed in a social world of relatively autonomous structures, including hierarchies. These condition vested interests and the disposition to promote or resist change. As with Mouzelis and Bourdieu, this explains the strongly tendential character of social life. But Archer does not 'relatively devalue the subjective moment'. Along with the variations arising from skill, knowledge and contingency, Archer maintains humanity's capacity for moral evaluation and acting against vested interests, and the irreducible uniqueness of persons. History is not 'rough' simply because of accidents, mistakes, incompetence and skill, but because people are a distinct natural kind capable of deliberately and rationally acting against the tendential forces generated by involuntary positioning. She steers between an over-socialized and an under-socialized conception of the person, maintaining the vital distinctions between *person* and *role* and the *sense of self* and *concepts of self*. These distinctions leave the relations open to variation and emergence. The autonomy of bodies with a continuous sense of self is 'the indispensable human element', the potential, upon which the social impinges. Though human beings are conditioned to become social beings their humanity is not a 'gift of society'. There has to be a presocial 'someone to do the becoming' (Archer 1995: 293).

The return of historical sociology

The post-'structurationists' want social theory to provide the concepts to guide the practical analysis of the structuration of events and relatively enduring patterns and institutions. For them structuration occurs in the relatively deep temporality of events and sequences, the time in which structures and agents can interact and produce their consequences. This zone between randomness and inevitability allows the constraining, conditioning, tendency-forming effects of structures to be predicted, though what actually happens depends on how agents respond to the structural conditions. Structuration is an *event-full* process. This is an explanatory method for a modest but valuable historical sociology of the emergence of specific developments.

However, historical sociology is not always so modest – as Giddens shows. In the grand style he tries to make the whole of human history intelligible, and in the process reveals the inadequacy of 'structuration' theory's concept of structure. This unfortunate outcome however does not rule out the possibility of grand historical sociology as such. Encouraged by Mouzelis's repeated endorsement of recent historical sociology of various degrees of 'grandness', one of the tasks of the next chapter is to consider if post-'structurationist' social theory is consistent with it.

9

Structuration and Historical Sociology

Introduction

This concluding chapter discusses the limits of the post-'structura-tionist' position first, by considering whether it is threatened by 'postmodernism'. Then it considers how Mann's and Runciman's neo-Weberian 'grand' historical sociology contributes to the under-standing of structuration, asking whether their approach is com-patible with that of the post-'structurationists'. Though not contributing directly to the debate about 'structuration' theory, Mann's and Runciman's success in accounting for structural development might have implications for it. The status of the post-'structurationists'' own programme for historical sociology depends on its ability to fend off a certain kind of postmodern critique and to establish a *modus vivendi* with other substantial achievements in the field.

My argument has been that (a) structuration is the basic problem of the social sciences; (b) social theory provides the basic concepts of social reality, governing what kinds of elements should figure in accounts of structuration; (c) the central problem of social theory is the relation between structure and agency; and (d) the post-'structurationist' dualistic relating of the two provides the most powerful explanatory methodology for use by practical social ana-lysts. These are all strong claims which, if true, make the achieve-ments of the post-'structurationists' very significant. Archer asserts that her position provides the basis for sociology in the next millennium and that the discipline may 'catch its second wind' on the basis of a 'tensed' relation between structure and agency (1998a: 84, 85). The relative lack of critical reaction suggests her analytical dualism may already be the new conventional wisdom (Healy 1998; King 1999; Zeuner 1999). The post-'structurationists' are part of a 'neo-traditionalist' recovery and revival of a sociological practice inspired by Max Weber's investigations of the uniqueness of western European development.

Relations with postmodernism

This book has focused on the problematic of structuration, looking at the debate about proposition (d) above, between those who accept claims (a)–(c). But the structuration problematic has also been implicated in 'postmodernism' – the wider movement to revise the legacy of modern social thought. Used broadly, postmodernism refers to ideas critical of 'modernism'. But since 'modernism' includes self-critical elements, no hard and fast distinction can be made between critical modernism and postmodernist critique. To the extent that reification and reduction are characteristic of 'modernist' social theory, 'structurationists' and post-'structurationists' are critical modernist or postmodernist. Post-'structurationists' reject modernization theory, systems functionalism and subjectivist individualism outright, while asserting the historical, emergent, objective character of social reality and the irreducibility of persons and agency. They abandon the positivist search for natural laws of progress and a predictive social science, in favour of retrodictive explanation in terms of the interplay of structural conditions and creative, strategic agency in 'open systems'. They see theoretically guided, analytic, genetic narratives of the appropriately periodized, sequential interplay of conditions and agency in specific places and times as the appropriate form for social scientific production.

However, theirs is a moderate kind of postmodernism. It maintains crucial elements from modernist social theory, namely objective social structures (avoiding reductionism), subjective actors (avoiding reification) and the possibility of a social science (avoiding relativism). These are the substantive commitments of the tradition they seek to revive. Thus the post-'structurationists' have had to extend their critique beyond 'structuration' theory, to include the postmodernist strain which wants to jettison all three: structures, subjects and science.

The unacceptable form of postmodern critique

Archer and Mouzelis defend their project against extreme post-modern critique. Though characteristically Mouzelis is more willing to explore what Archer dismisses as the result of a 'torrid affair with epistemology' (1998b: 193), they see the threat in the same terms and adopt a similar defence. To elaborate on the threat: by the 1960s the philosophy of social science had established that all knowledge depended on the use of concepts, that observational generalizations about correlations were not explanatory, and that one could not formulate predictive laws about societies because they were 'open systems' by virtue of being populated by creative human beings. The more radical postmodernists, however, took this acceptable and effective attack on empiricism and the old natural science model for social science to an unwarrantable 'extreme of relativism' (Mouzelis 1995: 49). They concluded that social knowledge could only consist of the internal relations among the concepts of the multitude of 'discourses', each its own 'incommensurable' arbiter of meaning, unconditioned by relations with whatever lay outside it. 'Knowledge dissolved into discourse', becoming thoroughly relativized, idealized, and removed from control by reference to the object world (Archer 1998a: 71).

Given the impossibility of determining any order in the world it thus remains radically indeterminate, 'fragile, chaotic, transient and discontinuous' (Mouzelis 1995: 42). 'Relatively durable social arrangements recede into the background or disappear altogether' (Mouzelis 1995: 59). The best that can be done on this basis is contemplatively to describe the 'multiplicity of local language games' (Archer 1998a: 71). The narratives of this 'new historicism' celebrate the uniqueness of identities, contexts and expression. Just like the 'old' historicism, 'each must be known by and for itself' (Parsons [1937]1968: 477). Without any epistemological context for justifying truth-claims, descriptions of such things can only be evaluated aesthetically. The theoretical justification of explanations and drawing out practical implications are redundant (Archer 1998a: 71–2). The condition of knowledge is made the condition of existence itself, as epistemology swallows up ontology (Archer

1998b: 195). Language and discourse become the substance of both knowledge and reality in a self-referring, narcissistic circle. Post-modernists turn out to be yet another band of conflationists, who 'completely fuse language and society', eliding knowledge and the object of knowledge (Mouzelis 1995: 58).

For the post-'structurationists' the antidote to the 'linguistic wrong turn' is the 'robust ontology' of a stratified reality of natural kinds, including social structure, agents and persons (Archer 1998b: 191–3). Reality is attributed to whatever exerts a causal force, enabling what is relational, detectable only through its effects, to be recognized as real. Social ontology defines the 'ultimate con-stituents' of social reality. 'The way things are in the world' limits what it is possible to say about it. One cannot, as some post-modernists imply, just say anything one likes. 'What is held to exist must exert an influence upon how it should be explained' (Archer 1998a: 72–3). Social ontology must regulate explanatory methodol-ogy. Language is *a* but not *the* condition of knowledge, since it must be used to refer to something other than itself. Both Archer and Mouzelis insist that empirical reference is a necessary condition for evaluation of the truth-claims upon which science depends. Social theory requires 'solid anchorage in an empirical reality' (Mouzelis 1995: 49). The concept-dependence of knowledge does not pre-clude arbitration between concepts and accepting that social reality imposes limits on its conceptualization. They fully agree with Giddens here (Giddens 1987: 62).

For Archer and Mouzelis, open systems prevent prediction but allow the retrodictive explanation of why, for specific cases, things turn out one way rather than another. Such explanations employ concepts of relatively enduring structural conditioning, interplay-ing with creative agency and the contingencies of context. Struc-tures are real constraining conditions of action, which cannot be grasped adequately by regarding them simply as effects of systems of representation or 'discourse'. The over-radical critique of social science removes the possibility of developing knowledge of the objective mechanisms inhibiting human emancipation. Post-modernism of this kind is politically and morally regressive. Non-utopian, neo-traditionalist social science offers the best hope for informing progressive political practice and feeding back into our efforts to elaborate the good life. Archer's programme is rational-ist, critical and humanist, standing four-square against the post-modern reduction of humanity to the status of a 'spongy referent, that opaque but equally translucent nothingness' (Archer 1998b: 193). There are no 'subjectless practices' (Mouzelis 1995: 45–8).

The 'mechanism' of history; social reality according to social realism

Archer and Mouzelis are social realists, trying to correct the 'incredible' claims of those postmodernists who deny social reality and the possibility of social science. The latter's explanations in terms of 'signs, texts, the unconscious or what have you' return social theory to a pre-Durkheimian condition (Mouzelis 1995: 54). The post-'structurationists'' defence of the possibility of a social science is grounded in a sense of the irreducible reality of objective social structures and their dependence on the action and interaction of structurally conditioned collectivities. As Archer puts it, 'The causal effects of the structures on individuals are manifested in certain structural interests, resources, powers, constraints and predicaments that are built into each position by the web of relationships' (Archer 1998b: 201–2). Without reference to 'collective actors (political, economic, religious etc.) and their intricate games and struggles over the distribution of resources and over the control of economic, political and cultural technologies' it is impossible to explain historical events or the conservation/transformation of patterns of advantage/disadvantage (Mouzelis 1995: 57). The historically productive interaction between struggling collectivities requires the conceptualization of relations constitutive of social 'wholes' at the 'macro' level. The interaction of structure and agency at the level at which collective agency is formed and operates explains the structuration of structures.

The reductionism (of both structure and agency) entailed by the forms of conflation typical of postmodernism and 'structuration' theory rules out tapping into the 'intricacies of institutional arrangements . . . the complex games actors play at a variety of hierarchical levels' (Mouzelis 1995: 59). Institutional and distributional positioning conditions agency by defining interests and access to resources. This means the stringency of constraint and the powers of agency vary from position to position. Against postmodernism and 'structuration' theory, the choice is not between fixed, unchangeable 'essences', on the one hand, and infinite, instant malleability on the other. Rather, fixity (constraint) and malleability (agency) vary in relation to the powers of hierarchized actors in particular times and places. The structuration of institutions and practices, that is to say their fragility/mutability or durability, depends on the way relatively autonomous agents use the resources structurally available to them (p. 61).

Explaining structuration in these terms demands facing the complexities of each historical case. There is a 'necessary historicity' in social explanation (Archer 1998b: 196). There are no 'lazy' alternatives to the painstaking investigation of the interaction between the relevant agents, structural conditions and contingencies (Mouzelis 1995: 57). Every case is unique, requiring its own narrative of the temporal process of its formation. Given the influence of contingency and that social structures are relatively enduring yet mutable, the explanation of each case requires 'an analytical history of its emergence, of why it is so and not otherwise' (Archer 1998b: 196). Each narrative will show how the openness of a system of relations became 'closed' on some event, or relatively enduring 'product', be it an institutional arrangement, configuration of power, a reconfigured network, a redistribution of privileges, an elaboration of a tradition etc. The meticulous analysis of the complexities of each case is not prevented by the structuration problematic (though it may be by 'structuration' theory) (Dean 1994: 7). The post-'structurationist' realists' dualistic relating of structure and agency requires such analysis. It does not reduce historical uniqueness but nor does it abandon the use of general social theory, as does postmodern 'new historicism'. Instead, particular narratives are constructed out of information assembled to determine the kinds of constraints and agents in play during the emergence of what is being investigated. Realist social theory guides, disciplines even, the research process and the construction of the appropriate narrative.

As social realists, the post-'structurationists' oppose the various forms of conflationary social theory by maintaining the irreducibility and autonomy of what goes on in the 'intermediate terrain' neglected by reified macro-teleological systematics and reductive individualism alike (Archer 1998c: 9–10). The dualist 'mechanism' of historical structuration can only produce relatively enduring structures which never become immutable. Fixity is always provisional, awaiting its transforming agency. 'Tales of trajectories are ever mutable. Struggles over the status quo shape whatever change does take place, thus generating a new context of action that again conditions but does not determine the future changes sought' (pp. 14–15). The activity-dependent and contingent character of the mechanism of change means that the future is open and guarantees nothing. Historical narratives, '*sans grandeur*', can do no more than give 'detailed analysis of the stringency of constraints for particular projects in specific contexts on the part of determinate groups, and the strategic use made of their respective degrees of freedom' (p. 15).

Analytical dualism and historical sociology

Dualist social realism demands that structuration be seen as the product of an intermediate level of reality, below any total system and above the individual. This generous zone (recognized and campaigned for by Marx, Durkheim and Weber) is where collectivization happens, as groups, corporate agents, networks, cultural traditions, institutions, hierarchies, games, alliances, stratification systems and struggles over the status quo are initiated, acquire their conditioning force, are maintained and transformed by agents. It is the zone of the relatively deep temporality of events and sequences where structures and agents interact, the zone of mutable tendencies and limited predictability, between randomness and inevitability. This is the object of Mouzelis's 'sociological theory proper', and Archer's sociological 'second wind'.

This 'second wind' is powerfully represented by contemporary historical sociology. Mann and Runciman offer accounts of historical development conforming to elements of the post-'structurationist' programme, but deal with the whole of human history and have an aura of grandeur that appears to deviate from it (Runciman 1983, 1989, 1995, 1997, 1998a, 1998b; Mann 1986, 1993; Callinicos 1995: 95–128). The issue their work raises is how comprehensive the account of history can be, based on the workings of the intermediate zone of collectivization and the contingent, temporal interplay of structure and agency. Giddens's 'structuration' theory did not support the directional element in his historical sociology. Now it is necessary to see if the post-'structuration' alternative is congruent with a historical sociology which makes claims about directionality.

Social realism is not a theory of history but has implications for what such a theory must be like (Callinicos 1995: 98–109). The fundamental question is whether, because social structures are mutable, largely unintended products of interaction and agency, subject to contingency, historical development is completely random. Postmodern 'new historicists', with their incredulity towards meta-narratives, and hostility to social theory, deny any meaning or directionality in history, thereby randomizing it. Randomness is all that is left if the only alternative to meta-narrative is theoretically undisciplined, aestheticized narration of unique instances, which cannot be conceptualized as examples or cases of anything more general than themselves.

However, the narrative enjoined by post-'structurationist' social realism is theoretically disciplined to give the detail of structure–agency interplay, which eventuates in the emergence of the object being accounted for. Though structures are mutable and have only power to condition agency, that conditioning power may be very substantial, quite sufficient to shape and limit the kinds of agents, their powers, opportunities and choices. In other words, the structural conditioning of agency creates developmental tendencies which, though in principle mutable, take time to change. This social theoretical principle means, at any given moment, change is possible, but not completely random. Some developments are more likely than others. Some may be virtually ruled out altogether. Though we cannot predict the future precisely, there are sufficient rational grounds for specifying a limited number of possibilities, and to that extent, offering a derandomized account of change. The intermediate zone, as I have called it, is one of limited, plural, but not random, directionality. It is the level at which one can specify alternative, possible tracks for future development, of the same logical order as the opportunity structures available to people located at different positions within distributional orders and institutions.

Such local, context-dependent prognosis about future change is not a theory of history. It does not provide any mechanism connecting the changes emerging within the multiplicity of 'open systems', which might explain the form that change has taken across the whole sweep of human existence. One would expect anyone who holds to dualist social realism to be discouraged from attempting such a 'grand' task. For example, Archer's account of the effects of the pre-existing distribution of literacy (a social structure) on moves to increase it in post-revolutionary Cuba is rather different from explaining why literacy has gradually but remorselessly spread round the globe as a 'world-historical' development (Archer 1982: 468–9). This sort of world-historical development is so extensive in time and space that it eludes its emergence being tracked at the 'intermediate' level. Yet Mann and Runciman attempt explanations of such scope, suggesting that despite the 'local' nature of emergence, there is nevertheless some overarching directionality to the development of social institutions and practices. What has to be identified is any theoretical implication, addition or extension required to enable post-'structurationist' social realism to support such a theory of history.

Mann and Runciman have different projects. Mann wants to provide the concepts to explain a specific historical development – the emergence by the nineteenth century of western Europe as the most powerful society yet seen. Runciman, on the other hand, develops the sociological categories for explaining historical development in general, producing a neo-evolutionary theory of history (Wickham 1988, 1991: 189; Anderson 1992: 76–86, 149–68). Nevertheless, their work shares two symptomatic features: historical comprehensiveness and a focus on power.

Given that non-teleological accounts of emergent structures or events are based on conditioned interaction, there is no *theoretical* limit to carrying the narrative of emergence back as far as it will go. The only constraints are practical, but a sufficiently ambitious historical sociologist can return to some starting point. Mann's explanation of the rise of Europe leads him to study the long-term development of social power, 'from the beginning'. Similarly, Runciman's evolutionary theory attempts to explain all change from the earliest forms of social organization. The post-'structurationist' position does not rule out this ambitiousness, since there are no strict criteria for delimiting the historical context deemed relevant for producing analytical narratives. However, setting context wide and deep risks losing, or making mistakes about, the essential detail convincing narratives demand. But these are technical problems, which do not invalidate the enterprise in principle. From social realism's perspective, Mann's and Runciman's ambition is legitimate though extremely difficult to achieve.

Mann's and Runciman's focus on power in their accounts of structuration follows from their view of social structures. Runciman sees three kinds of power derived from access to or control of the means of production, means of persuasion, or means of coercion (1989: 12). The study of society is 'the study of people in roles, and the study of people in roles is the study of the institutional distribution of power' (p. 3). The three kinds of power are universal because human beings are susceptible to being controlled through their relations with material production, ideas and violence. So institutional structures distribute power to some roles enabling their occupants to dominate others. Similarly Mann sees the relative fixity of social orders as the product of agents' use of four kinds of power networks (ideological, economic, military, political) to constrain people's action and integrate spaces within power relations (1986: 2). Each kind of social power in his 'IEMP model' is 'necessary to social existence and to each other' (1993: 7–10). Minor differences in conceptualizing power aside, both theorists explain structures in terms of the requirements for establishing, maintaining and transforming relations of domination. Structures are the products of the domination struggles of agents. Social power is the capacity to produce institutions, regularities and patterns in the lives of other people. Mann refers to this as 'social caging'. This is consistent with Mouzelis's and Archer's view of the structuration process. 'If the damned things [social structures] are patterned, it is because real men and women impose patterns. They attempt to control the world and increase their rewards within it by setting up power organisations of varying ... strengths' (Mann 1986: 532). The intermediate zone accounts for the 'wild zig-zag' between stability and change as 'social groups struggle to wrest the [steering] wheel from one another' (Archer 1998a: 75).

History has no final destination and the future course of social development is unpredictable. Mann asserts that 'the "might have beens" and "almost weres" could have led into fundamentally different historical tracks' and that 'power struggles are the principal patternings of history but their outcomes have often been close run' (Mann 1986: 531). For Runciman, 'Evolution is movement away from, rather than towards' (1989: 297). So accounting for why Europe ended up as it was, say, on the eve of the First World War entails travelling back through time, identifying the crises, watersheds, battles, decisions by the powerful, thresholds, all those 'switching points' where things might have gone differently. In Mann's case this takes him back, for example, to the establishment, by 1000 A.D., of western Europe as 'Christendom', unified ideologically by a religion which overarched a 'multi-power actor network' of competing states, thereby creating unique conditions for increasing power. Western European 'Christendom' in turn leads back to the Christianizing of the Roman Empire, and then ultimately to the very earliest forms of state, which 'caged' their populations by making them dependent on centrally administered irrigation systems (Mann 1986). In Runciman's terms, there can only be accounts of the development of the 'winners' of particular struggles in the unending competition for dominance and power, and these must not presuppose 'that their success was foreseeable' (1989: 40). Social development has only the direction it *has* taken, not one it *will* take.

Yet Mann and Runciman do generalize about historical development, suggesting there is more to the process of structuration than the contingent interplay of structure and agency where, in principle, anything can happen. Historical development shows that 'Seen in the very long run, the infrastructure available to power holders and to societies at large has steadily increased. Many different societies have contributed to this. But, once invented, the major infrastructural techniques seem almost never to have disappeared from human practice' (Mann 1986: 524–7). Literacy is an example of a social invention that, once gained, has been retained and has crucially increased power capacities (Mann 1986: 525). For Runciman there has been 'progression towards more and more complex forms of social organisation' (1989: 39). Both claim that what Mann calls the 'infrastructural techniques of power', and Runciman 'functionally superior practices which give competitive advantage', somehow *accumulate* to increase complexity and power. Relations between the post-'structurationists' and this type of historical sociology hang on their accounts of the mechanisms of accumulation.

Runciman's explanation for increasing complexity is simply that new practices conferring competitive advantage do not necessarily displace older ones (1989: 39–40). Given time, complexity results from multiplying the range of coexisting forms. Further, the mutation and recombination of practices is unpredictable, driven by the search for competitive advantage (p. 42). Runciman insists his version of evolutionism, where change is the product of the competitive selection of practices, entails no vicious teleology, since it allows that 'newer forms progressively supersede the old [and that] the range of forms progressively widens', because older forms are retained (p. 39). This 'directionality' is an incidental and unsurprising by-product of social competition. It does not steer the course of history in teleological fashion, only showing the path that has been trod. The universal of social competition, rather than inevitably increasing complexity, explains the course of history.

Mann's more complex account of the long-term accumulation of

increasingly effective techniques of social power is less easily summarized. But in essence it is an inevitable effect of relations of
domination and competition. Both the dominant and subordinate
within networks of power have interests in developing effective
methods of control and /or its evasion. Moreover, because such networks are relatively unbounded structures of interaction, even the
most powerful of them leave room for the development of alternative, 'interstitial' power networks, by those most loosely 'caged',
and opportunities to invent new techniques which alter power
distribution. Lastly, external competitors will be interested in any
new advantageous techniques (Mann 1986: 17–32). As with Runciman, this kind of 'progress' or direction is not a motor of change
but the systematic by-product of people entangled in power
relations 'striving to increase their enjoyment of the good things of
life and capable of choosing and pursuing appropriate means for
doing so' (Mann 1986: 4).

This brief encounter with some of the most important recent historical sociology shows it to be consistent with the dualistic understanding of the relation between structure and agency. Agents are
conditioned and struggle to change those conditions. Sociology
should aspire to provide the sort of substantive insight into the
structuration process provided by Mann and Runciman. And since
such work requires a conceptualization of structure and agency's
relation, then it has to be one of dualism. Once the argument for
the necessity of dualism has been won, as it surely has, the concept
of structuration can be dissociated from the dead-end of 'structuration' theory, and sociologists can, and should, get on with what
they are good at, namely producing substantive historico-genetic
narratives of varying degrees of ambitiousness.

Bibliography

Starred items are particularly significant.

Abercrombie, N. *et al.* (1980) *The Dominant Ideology Thesis*. London: Allen & Unwin.

Alexander, J. C. (1995) *Fin de Siècle Social Theory*. London: Verso.

Anderson, P. (1983) *In the Tracks of Historical Materialism*. London: Verso.

Anderson, P. (1990) 'A culture in contraflow, 1', *New Left Review*, 180: 41–78.

Anderson, P. (1992) *A Zone of Engagement*. London: Verso.

Antonio, R. J. and Kellner, D. (1994) 'The future of social theory and the limits of postmodern critique', in D. R. Dickens and A. Fontana (eds) *Postmodernism and Social Inquiry*. London: UCL Press.

Archer, M. S. (1979) *Social Origins of Educational Systems*. London: Sage.

*Archer, M. S. (1982) 'Morphogenesis versus structuration: on combining structure and agency', *British Journal of Sociology*, 33(4): 455–83.

Archer, M. S. (1983) 'Process without system', *European Journal of Sociology*, 24(1): 196–221.

Archer, M. S. (1988) *Culture and Agency*. Cambridge: Cambridge University Press.

Archer, M. S. (1990) 'Human agency and social structure: a critique of Giddens', in J. Clark, C. Modgil and S. Modgil (eds) *Anthony Giddens: Consensus and Controversy*. Basingstoke: Falmer Press.

Archer, M. S. (1993) 'Bourdieu's theory of cultural reproduction: French or universal?', *French Cultural Studies*, (iv): 225–40.

*Archer, M. S. (1995) *Realist Social Theory: A Morphogenetic Approach*. Cambridge: Cambridge University Press.

Archer, M. S. (1996) 'Social integration and system integration: developing the distinction', *Sociology*, 30(4): 679–99.

*Archer, M. S. (1998a) 'Social theory and the analysis of society', in T. May, and M. Williams (eds) *Knowing the Social World*. Buckingham: Open University Press.

Archer, M. S. (1998b) 'Introduction: realism in the social sciences', in M. S. Archer, R. Bhaskar, A. Collier, T. Lawson and A. Norrie (eds) *Critical Realism*. London: Routledge.

Archer, M. S. (1998c) 'The dubious guarantees of social science', *International Sociology*, 13(1): 5–17.

Atkinson, D. (1971) *Orthodox Consensus and Radical Alternative*. London: Heinemann.

Avineri, S. (1968) *The Social and Political Thought of Karl Marx*. Cambridge: Cambridge University Press.

Baert, P. (1998) *Social Theory in the Twentieth Century*. Cambridge: Polity.

Barbalet, J. (1987) 'Structural Resources and Agency', *Current Perspectives in Social Theory*, 8: 1–24.

Barrell, J. (1983) *English Literature in History 1730–80: An Equal Wide survey*. London: Hutchinson.

*Bauman, Z. (1989) 'Hermeneutics and modern social theory', in D. Held and J. B. Thompson (eds) *Social Theory of Modern Societies: Anthony Giddens and his Critics*. Cambridge: Cambridge University Press.

Benton, T. (1984) *The Rise and Fall of Structuralist Marxism*. London: Macmillan.

Berger, P. and Luckmann, T. (1966) *The Social Construction of Reality*. Harmondsworth: Penguin.

Bernstein, R. J. (1976) *The Restructuring of Social and Political Theory*. Oxford: Blackwell.

Bershady, H. (1973) *Ideology and Social Knowledge*. Oxford: Blackwell.

*Bottomore, T. and Rubel, M. (eds) (1961) *Karl Marx: Selected Writings in Sociology and Philosophy*. Harmondsworth: Penguin.

*Bourdieu, P. ([1972]1977) *Outline of a Theory of Practice*. Cambridge: Cambridge University Press.

Bourdieu, P. ([1980]1990) *The Logic of Practice*. Cambridge: Polity.

*Bourdieu, P. (1981) 'Men and machines', in K. Knorr-Cetina and A. V. Cicourel (eds) *Advances in Social Theory and Methodology*. London: Routledge and Kegan Paul.

Bourdieu, P. ([1984]1988) *Homo Academicus*. Cambridge: Polity.

Bourdieu, P. (1985) 'The genesis of the concepts of habitus and field', *Sociocriticism*, 2: 11–24.

Bourdieu, P. (1986) 'From rules to strategies', *Cultural Anthropology*, 1: 110–20.

Bourdieu, P. (1987) 'Legitimation and structural interests in Weber's sociology of religion', in S. Whimster and S. Lash (eds) *Max Weber, Rationality and Modernity*. London: Allen & Unwin.

Bourdieu, P. (1988) 'Vive la crise! For heterodoxy in social science', *Theory and Society*, 17(5): 773–87.

Bourdieu, P. (1990) *In Other Words*. Cambridge: Polity.

Bourdieu, P. (1993) *The Field of Cultural Production*. Cambridge: Polity.

Bourdieu, P. (1998) *Practical Reason*. Cambridge: Polity.

*Bourdieu, P. and Waquant, L. (1992) *An Invitation to Reflexive Sociology*. Cambridge: Polity.

Boyne, R. (1993) 'Pierre Bourdieu and the question of the subject', *French Cultural Studies*, 4.3(12): 241–51.

Buckley, W. (1967) *Sociology and Modern Systems Theory*. Englewood Cliffs, NJ: Prentice-Hall.

Bulmer, M. ed. (1975) *Working-class Images of Society*. London: Routledge and Kegan Paul.

Burkitt, I. (1991) *Social Selves*. London: Sage.

Calhoun, C. (1993) 'Habitus, field and capital: historical specificity in the theory of practice', in C. Calhoun *et al.* (eds) *Bourdieu: Critical Perspectives*. Cambridge: Polity.

Callinicos, A. (1985) 'Anthony Giddens – a contemporary critique', *Theory and Society*, 14(2): 133–66.

Callinicos, A. (1989) *Making History*. Cambridge: Polity.

Callinicos, A. (1995) *Theories and Narratives*. Cambridge: Polity.

Callinicos, A. (1999) 'Social theory put to the test of politics: Pierre Bourdieu and Anthony Giddens', *New Left Review*, 236: 77–102.

Casper, M. J. (1994) 'Reframing and grounding nonhuman agency: what makes a fetus an agent', *American Behavioral Scientist* 37(6): 839–56.

Clarke, S. (1981) *The Foundations of Structuralism*. Brighton: Harvester.

Clegg, S. (1992) 'How to become an internationally famous British social theorist', *Sociological Review*, 40(3): 576–98.

Cohen, I. J. (1996) 'Theories of action and praxis', in B. S. Turner (ed.) *The Blackwell Companion to Social Theory*. Oxford: Blackwell.

*Craib, I. (1986) 'Back to Utopia: Anthony Giddens and modern social theory', *Radical Philosophy*, 43: 17–21.

Craib, I. (1992a) *Modern Social Theory*, 2nd edition. Hemel Hempstead: Harvester.

Craib, I. (1992b) *Anthony Giddens*. London: Routledge.

*Crowther, P. (1994) 'Sociological Imperialism and the field of cultural production: the case of Bourdieu', *Theory, Culture and Society*, 11(1): 155–69.

*Dahrendorf, R. (1958) 'Out of Utopia: towards a reorientation of sociological analysis', *American Journal of Sociology*, lxiv(2): 115–27.

Dahrendorf, R. (1959) *Class and Class Conflict in an Industrial Society*. London: Routledge and Kegan Paul.

*Dawe, A. (1970) 'The two sociologies', *British Journal of Sociology*, 21(2): 207–18.

Dawe, A. (1978) 'Theories of social action', in T. Bottomore and R. Nisbet (eds) *A History of Sociological Analysis*. New York, NY: Basic Books.

Dean, M. (1994) *Critical and Effective Histories: Foucault's Methods and Historical Sociology*. London: Routledge.

Demerath, N. J. and Petersen, R. A. (eds) (1967) *System, Change and Conflict*. New York, NY: The Free Press.

DiTomaso, N. (1982) 'Sociological reductionism from Parsons to Althusser: linking action and structure in social theory', *American Sociological Review*, 47(1): 14–28.

Fowler, B. (1997) *Pierre Bourdieu and Cultural Theory*. London: Sage.

Fuller, S. (1994) 'Making agency count: a brief foray into the foundations of social theory', *American Behavioural Scientist*, 37(6): 741–53.

Fuller, S. (1998a) 'From content to context: a social epistemology of the structure–agency craze', in A. Sica (ed.) *What is Social Theory?* Oxford: Blackwell.

Fuller, S. (1998b) 'Divining the future of social theory: from theology to rhetoric via social epistemology', *European Journal of Social Theory*, 1(1): 107–26.

Garfinkel, H. (1967) *Studies in Ethnomethodology*. Englewood Cliffs, NJ: Prentice-Hall.

*Gellner, E. (1956) 'Holism versus individualism', in M. Brodbeck (ed.) (1971) *Readings in the Philosophy of the Social Sciences*. New York, NY: Collier MacMillan.

Giddens, A. (1971) *Capitalism and Modern Social Theory*. Cambridge: Cambridge University Press.

Giddens, A. (1973) *The Class Structure of the Advanced Societies*. London: Hutchinson.

Giddens, A. (ed.) (1974) *Positivism and Sociology*. London: Heinemann.

*Giddens, A. (1976) *New Rules of Sociological Method*. London: Hutchinson.

Giddens, A. (1977) 'Functionalism: Aprés La Lutte', in A. Giddens (ed.) *Studies in Social and Political Theory*. London: Hutchinson.

*Giddens, A. (1979) *Central Problems in Social Theory*. London: Macmillan.

Giddens, A. (1981a) *A Contemporary Critique of Historical Materialism*. London: Macmillan.

Giddens, A. (1981b) 'Agency, institution, and time–space analysis', in K. Knorr-Cetina and A. Cicourel (eds) *Advances in Social Theory and Methodology*. London: Routledge and Kegan Paul.

Giddens, A. (1982) *Profiles and Critiques in Social Theory*. London: Macmillan.

*Giddens, A. (1984) *The Constitution of Society*. Cambridge: Polity.

Giddens, A. (1986) 'The politics of taste', *Partisan Review*, 53(2): 300–3.

Giddens, A. (1987) *Social Theory and Modern Sociology*. Cambridge: Polity.

Giddens, A. (1990a) *The Consequences of Modernity*. Cambridge: Polity.

Giddens, A. (1990b) 'Structuration theory and sociological analysis', in J. Clark, C. Modgil and S. Modgil (eds) *Anthony Giddens: Consensus and Controversy*. Basingstoke: Falmer.

Giddens, A. (1991) *Modernity and Self-identity*. Cambridge: Polity.

Giddens, A. (1994) *Beyond Left and Right*. Cambridge: Polity.

Giddens, A. (1996) *In Defence of Sociology*. Cambridge: Polity.

Giddens, A. and Pierson, C. (1998) *Conversations with Anthony Giddens*. Cambridge: Polity.

Goldthorpe, J. H., Lockwood, D., Bechhofer, F., and Platt, J. (1968–9) *The Affluent Worker*, Vols 1–3. Cambridge: Cambridge University Press.

Gouldner, A. (1970) *The Coming Crisis of Western Sociology*. London: Heinemann.

Gouldner, A. (1980) *The Two Marxisms*. London: Macmillan.

Gregory, D. (1989) 'Presences and absences: time-space relations and structuration theory', in D. Held and J. B. Thompson (eds) *Social Theory of Modern Societies: Anthony Giddens and his Critics*. Cambridge: Polity.

*Healy, K. (1998) 'Conceptualising constraint: Mouzelis, Archer and the concept of social structure', *Sociology*, 32(3): 509–22.

Homans, G. (1964) 'Bring men back in', *American Sociological Review*, 29(6): 809–18.

Honneth, A. (1986) 'The fragmented world of symbolic forms: reflections on Pierre Bourdieu's sociology of culture', *Theory, Culture and Society*, 3(3): 55–66.

Hughes, J., Martin, P. J. and Sharrock, W. W. (1995) *Understanding Classical Sociology*. London: Sage.

Jary, D. (1991) ' "Society as a time-traveller": Giddens on historical change, historical materialism and the nation-state in world society', in C. G. A. Bryant and D. Jary (eds) *Giddens' Theory of Structuration: A Critical Appreciation*. London: Routledge.

Jenkins, R. (1992) *Pierre Bourdieu*. London: Routledge.

*Kalberg, S. (1994) *Max Weber's Comparative Historical Sociology*. Cambridge: Polity.

*Kilminster, K. (1991) 'Structuration theory as a world view', in C. G. A. Bryant and D. Jary (eds) *Giddens' Theory of Structuration: A Critical Appreciation*. London: Routledge.

King, A. (1999) 'Against structure: a critique of morphogenetic social theory', *Sociological Review*, 47(2): 199–227.

Lash, S. (1990) *The Sociology of Postmodernism*. London: Routledge.

Layder, D. (1981) *Structure, Interaction and Social Theory*. London: Routledge and Kegan Paul.

Layder, D. (1987) 'Key issues in structuration theory', *Current Perspectives in Social Theory*, 8: 25–46.

Layder, D. (1994) *Understanding Social Theory*. London: Sage.

Layder, D. (1996) 'Review essay: contemporary social theory', *Sociology*, 3(3): 601–8.

Layder, D. (1997) *Modern Social Theory: Key Debates and New Directions*. London: UCL Press.

Layder, D. (1998) 'The reality of social domains: implications for theory and methods', in *T. May and M. Williams (eds) *Knowing the Social World*. Buckingham: Open University Press.

Lee, N. (1998) 'Towards an immature sociology', *Sociological Review*, 46(3): 458–82.

*Lockwood, D. (1964) 'Social integration and system integration', in G. Zollschan and H. Hirsch (eds) *Explorations in Social Change*. London: Routledge and Kegan Paul.

Lockwood, D. (1966) 'Sources of variation in working-class images of society', *Sociological Review*, 14(3): 249–67.

*Lockwood, D. (1981) 'The weakest link in the chain? Some comments on the Marxist theory of action', in D. Rose (ed.) (1988) *Social Stratification and Economic Change*. London: Hutchinson.

Lockwood, D. (1992) *Solidarity and Schism: 'The Problem of Disorder' in Durkheimian and Marxist Sociology*. Oxford: Clarendon Press.

McLennan, G. (1995) 'After postmodernism – back to sociological theory?', *Sociology*, 29(1): 117–32.

McLennan, G. (1998) 'Fin de sociology?: The dilemmas of multidimensional sociology', *New Left Review*, 230: 58–90.

Mann, M. (1970) 'The social cohesion of liberal democracy', *American Sociological Review*, 35(3): 423–39.

Mann, M. (1973) *Consciousness and Action in the Western Working Class*. London: Macmillan.

*Mann, M. (1986) *The Sources of Social Power*, Volume 1. Cambridge: Cambridge University Press.

Mann, M. (1988) *States, War and Capitalism*. Oxford: Blackwell.

Mann, M. (1993) *The Sources of Social Power*, Volume 2. Cambridge: Cambridge University Press.

Mann, M. (1995) 'Sources of variation in working-class movements in twentieth-century Europe', *New Left Review*, 212: 14–54.

Mann, M. (1999) 'The dark side of democracy: the modern tradition of ethnic and political cleansing', *New Left Review*, 235: 18–45.

Marx, K. ([1857–8]1964) *Pre-Capitalist Economic Formations*, translated by E. J. Hobsbaum. London: Lawrence and Wishart.

Marx, K. and Engels, F. ([1846]1965) *The German Ideology*. London: Lawrence and Wishart.

Marx, K. ([1857–8]1973) *Grundrisse*, translated by M. Nicolaus. Harmondsworth: Penguin.

May, T. (1996) *Situating Social Theory*. Buckingham: Open University Press.

Mead, G. H. (1934) *Mind, Self and Society*. Chicago, IL: University of Chicago Press.

*Merton, R. K. (1957) *Social Theory and Social Structure*. New York, NY: The Free Press.

Mouzelis, N. (1967) *Organisation and Bureaucracy*. London: Routledge and Kegan Paul.

Mouzelis, N. (1974) 'System and social integration: a reconsideration of a fundamental distinction', in N. Mouzelis (1991) *Back to Sociological Theory*, Ch. 3. Basingstoke: Macmillan.

Mouzelis, N. (1975) *Organisation and Bureaucracy*, 2nd edition. London: Routledge and Kegan Paul.

Mouzelis, N. (1978) *Modern Greece*. Basingstoke: Macmillan.

Mouzelis, N. (1980) 'Types of reductionism in Marxist theory', in N. Mouzelis (1990) *Post-Marxist Alternatives*, Appendix 1. Basingstoke: Macmillan.

Mouzelis, N. (1986) *Politics in the Semi-periphery: Early Parliamentarianism and Late Industrialisation in the Balkans and Latin America*. Basingstoke: Macmillan.

Mouzelis, N. (1988) 'Marxism versus Post-Marxism', in N. Mouzelis (1990) *Post-Marxist Alternatives*, Ch. 2. Basingstoke: Macmillan.

Mouzelis, N. (1989) 'Restructuring structuration theory', in N. Mouzelis (1991) *Back to Sociological Theory*, Ch. 2. Basingstoke: Macmillan.

Mouzelis, N. (1990) *Post-Marxist Alternatives*. Basingstoke: Macmillan.

*Mouzelis, N. (1991) *Back to Sociological Theory*. Basingstoke: Macmillan.

Mouzelis, N. (1992) 'The interaction order and the micro–macro distinction', *Sociological Theory*, 10(1): 122–8.

Mouzelis, N. (1993) 'Comparing the Durkheimian and the Marxist traditions', *Sociological Review*, 41(3): 572–82.

*Mouzelis, N. (1995) *Sociological Theory: What Went Wrong?* London: Routledge.

Mouzelis, N. (1996) 'After post-modernism: a reply to Gregor McLennan', *Sociology*, 30(1): 133–5.

Mouzelis, N. (1997a) 'Social and system integration: Lockwood, Habermas, Giddens', *Sociology*, 31(1): 111–19.

Mouzelis, N. (1997b) 'In defence of the sociological canon: a reply to David Parker', *Sociological Review*, 45(2): 244–53.

New, C. (1994) 'Structure, agency and social transformation', *Journal for the Study of Social Behaviour*, 24(3): 187–205.

Ollman, B. (1971) *Alienation*. Cambridge: Cambridge University Press.

*Parsons, T. ([1937]1968) *The Structure of Social Action*. New York, NY: The Free Press.

*Parsons, T. (1966) *Societies*. Englewood Cliffs, NJ: Prentice-Hall.

Parsons, T. (1971) *The System of Modern Societies*. Engelwood Cliffs, NJ: Prentice-Hall.

Poggi, G. (1990) *The State*. Cambridge: Polity.

Porpora, D. V. (1989) 'Four concepts of social structure', in M. S. Archer, R. Bhaskar, A. Collier, T. Lawson and A. Norrie (eds) (1998) *Critical Realism*. London: Routledge.

Rex, J. (1961) *Key Problems in Sociological Theory*. London: Routledge and Kegan Paul.

*Runciman, W. G. (1983) *A Treatise on Social Theory*, Volume 1. Cambridge: Cambridge University Press.

*Runciman, W. G. (1989) *A Treatise on Social Theory*, Volume 2. Cambridge: Cambridge University Press.

Runciman, W. G. (1995) 'The "triumph" of capitalism as a topic in the theory of social selection', *New Left Review*, 210: 33–47.

*Runciman, W. G. (1997) *A Treatise on Social Theory, Volume 3*. Cambridge: Cambridge University Press.

*Runciman, W. G. (1998a) 'The selectionist paradigm and its implications for sociology', *Sociology*, 32(1): 163–88.

Runciman, W. G. (1998b) *The Social Animal*. London: Harper Collins.

Runciman, W. G. (1999) 'Social evolutionism: a reply to Michael Rustin', *New Left Review*, 236: 145–53.

Runciman, W. G., Maynard Smith, J. and Dunbar, R. I. M. (eds) (1996) *The Evolution of Social Behaviour Patterns in Primates and Man*. Oxford: Oxford University Press.

Rustin, M. (1999) 'A new social evolutionism?' *New Left Review*, 234: 106–26.

Sayer, A. (1992) *Method in Social Science: A Realist Approach*. London: Routledge.

Schutz, A. ([1932]1967) *The Phenomenology of the Social World*. Evanston, Ill: Northwestern University Press.

Schutz, A. (1964–67) *Collected Papers*, Vols 1–3. The Hague: Martin Nijhoff.

Scott, J. (1995) *Sociological Theory*. Aldershot: Edward Elgar.

Sewell, W.H. (1997) 'Three temporalities: towards an eventful sociology' in T. J. McDonald (ed.) *The Historical Turn in the Human Sciences*. Ann Arbor, MI: University of Michigan Press.

Sjoberg, G. (1960) 'Contradictory functional requirements and social systems', *Conflict Resolution*, 4(2): 198–208.

Soper, K. (1986) *Humanism and Anti-humanism*. London: Hutchinson.

Steinmetz, G. (1998) 'Critical realism and historical sociology', *Comparative Studies in Society and History*, 40(1): 170–86.

Taylor, C. (1993) 'To follow a rule . . .', in C. Calhoun *et al.* (eds) *Bourdieu: Critical Perspectives*. Cambridge: Polity.

Thompson, E. P. (1963) *The Making of the English Working Class*. Harmondsworth: Penguin.

Thompson, J. B. (1984) *Studies in the Theory of Ideology*. Cambridge: Polity.

*Thompson, J. B. (1989) 'The theory of structuration', in D. Held and J. B. Thompson (eds) *Social Theory of Modern Societies: Anthony Giddens and his Critics*. Cambridge: Cambridge University Press.

Thompson, J.B. (1991) 'Introduction', in P. Bourdieu *Language and Symbolic Power*. Cambridge: Polity.

Tucker, K. H. (1998) *Anthony Giddens and Modern Social Theory*. London: Sage.

*Watkins, J. W. N. (1957) 'Methodological individualism and social tendencies', in Brodbeck, M. (ed.) (1971) *Readings in the Philosophy of the Social Sciences*. New York, NY: Collier MacMillan.

Weber, M. (1967) *From Max Weber*, edited by H. Gerth and C. W. Mills. London: Routledge and Kegan Paul.

Weber, M. (1968) *Economy and Society*, edited by G. Roth and C. Wittich. NY: Bedminster Press.

Wickham, C. J. (1988) 'Historical materialism, historical sociology', *New Left Review*, 171: 63–78.

Wickham, C. J. (1991) 'Systactic structures: social theory for historians', *Past and Present*, 132: 188–203.

Williams, R. (1983) *Keywords*. London: Fontana.

Wright, E. O. (1989) 'Models of historical trajectory: an assessment of Giddens's critique of Marxism', in D. Held and J. B. Thompson (eds) *Social Theory of Modern Societies: Anthony Giddens and his Critics*. Cambridge: Cambridge University Press.

Wright, E. O., Levine, A. and Sober, E. (1992) *Recontructing Marxism*. London: Verso.

*Wrong, D. (1961) 'The oversocialized conception of man in modern sociology', *American Sociological Review*, xxvi (2): 184–93.

Zeuner, L. (1999) 'Margaret Archer on structural and cultural morphogenesis', *Acta Sociologica*, 42(1): 79–86.

Zimmerman, D. (1971) 'The practicalities of rule use', in J. D. Douglas (ed.) *Understanding Everyday Life*. London: Routledge and Kegan Paul.

Index